# Edexcel GCSE
# Physical Education

**Maarit Edy and
Matthew Hunter**

# Contents

# HEALTH AND PERFORMANCE

# PRACTICAL APPLICATION

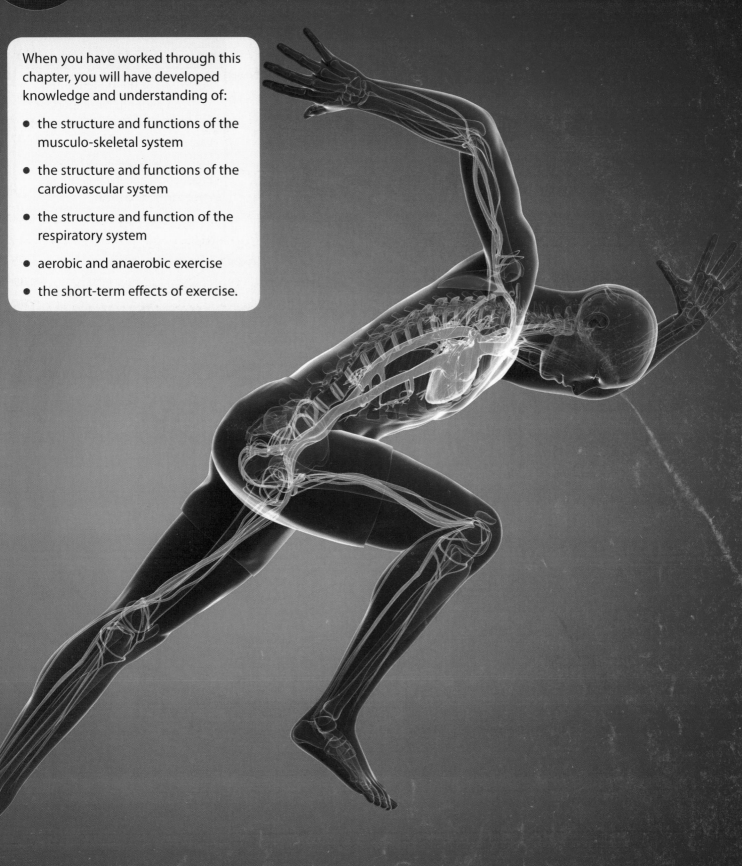

# Applied anatomy and physiology

When you have worked through this chapter, you will have developed knowledge and understanding of:

- the structure and functions of the musculo-skeletal system
- the structure and functions of the cardiovascular system
- the structure and function of the respiratory system
- aerobic and anaerobic exercise
- the short-term effects of exercise.

The skeletal system is made up of many bones with different classifications. While all bones have things in common, the structure of each type of bone allows it to fulfil one or more of the **functions of the skeleton.**

## Protection of vital organs

Many bones act as a rigid shell. They protect vital organs and the central nervous system, which are soft and easily damaged. During physical activity, protection is crucial for both performance and long-term health. It reduces the chance of injury, which ensures players can continue to train and play. Examples include the cranium protecting the brain, and the spinal column protecting the spinal cord.

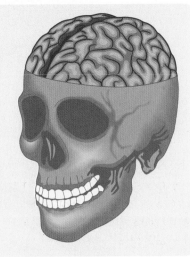

**Functions of the skeleton**

## Muscle attachment

Bones provide a surface for muscles to attach to via tendons. When muscles contract, movement is achieved. The ability to move is central to all physical activities, and movements are created by muscles. For example, the biceps muscle attaches to the radius and ulna in the forearm, and when it contracts your elbow flexes.

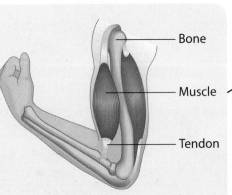

Bone

Muscle

Tendon

## Joints for movement

A joint is a place where two or more bones meet and allow movement to take place. Joints – and the movements they allow – are crucial in the performance of physical activities. Whether flexing your elbow or extending your knee, all sporting actions require muscles to manipulate bones at joints. Without joints, you would not move.

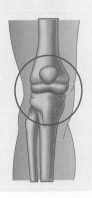

## Blood cell production

Red blood cells, white blood cells, and platelets are produced in bone marrow contained within certain bones. Red blood cells are especially important in aerobic activities because they carry oxygen to working muscles. White blood cells fight off infections, and platelets help blood to clot following an injury.

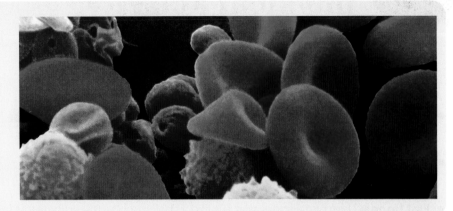

## Mineral storage

Calcium and phosphorus, along with other minerals, are stored within the bones. These minerals are necessary for vital body functions. For example, calcium and phosphorus are both needed for strong teeth and bones, while calcium is involved in muscular contractions. Their role in physical activity is, therefore, linked to the general health of an athlete, which clearly affects sporting performance.

## Activities

1   Look at this photograph and discuss how the different functions of the skeleton are important in rugby.

2   In a group, write down ten sports or physical activities on separate scraps of paper and put them in a hat. Take it in turns to pick an activity out of the hat and give specific examples of how each function of the skeleton is important in the activity you selected.

# Bone classifications and physical activity

There are four major **classifications of bone** in the human skeleton.

- **Long bones:** Bones that are longer than they are wide, like a femur. These play a key part in leverage and movement.

- **Short bones:** Bones that are box-like in shape, like tarsals. These are designed to be weight bearing.

- **Flat bones:** Thin, plate bones that act like a shell, such as the cranium. They provide protection and a large surface to which muscles can attach.

- **Irregular bones:** Unusually shaped bones for a unique purpose, like vertebrae. These also provide protection and a large surface to which muscles can attach.

> ### Key term
>
> **Classifications of bone:** The bone classification tells you a lot about its structure. A bone's classification will also link closely to its major functions.

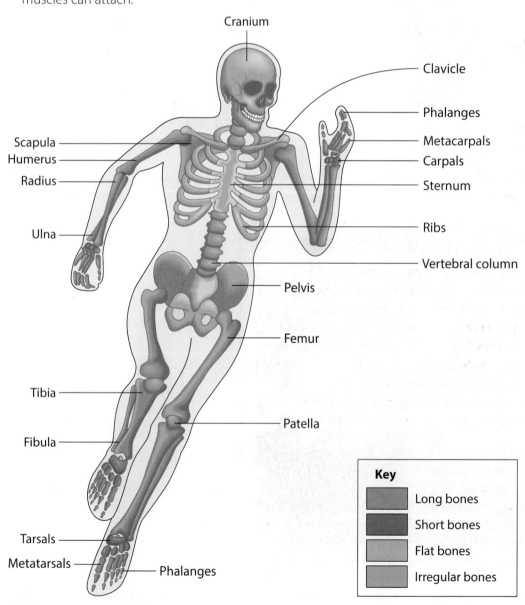

Cranium

Clavicle

Phalanges

Metacarpals

Carpals

Sternum

Ribs

Vertebral column

Scapula

Humerus

Radius

Ulna

Pelvis

Femur

Tibia

Patella

Fibula

Tarsals

Metatarsals

Phalanges

**Key**
- Long bones
- Short bones
- Flat bones
- Irregular bones

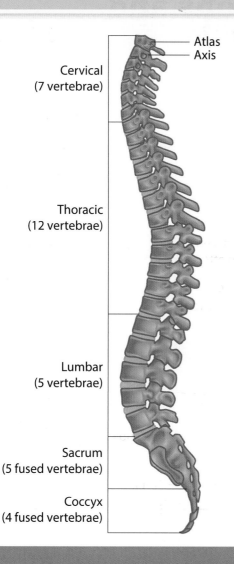

Atlas
Axis

Cervical
(7 vertebrae)

Thoracic
(12 vertebrae)

Lumbar
(5 vertebrae)

Sacrum
(5 fused vertebrae)

Coccyx
(4 fused vertebrae)

## Activity

**3** **a)** It is important to be able to classify a bone and describe its function
linked to physical activity and sport. This activity will help you to
practise this. Take four sticky labels. On each one, write down the
name of a bone, its classification, its major function and a sporting
example illustrating the bone fulfilling its function. Do one label for
each type of bone, then stick the labels on yourself to show that you
know where each bone is located. For example: *The humerus is a
long bone which is very important for leveraging the arm. The way the
humerus acts as a lever can be seen when an athlete throws a javelin.*

**b)** Now write out all the other bone names, including the five separate
regions of the vertebral column, on separate sticky labels. Study the
skeleton diagram for a few minutes. Place all the labels face down on
the table and then, with a partner, take it in turns to take a label and
stick it on yourself in the correct place. Check back in the book to see
if you're correct. Each correct placement earns you a point. If you're
incorrect, put it back on the table and mix up the labels before the
next go.

# Joint classifications and physical activity

A joint is defined as a place where two or more bones meet.

Bones are rigid so it is the presence of joints that allows movements to occur. Most joints in the human body are freely movable or "synovial" joints. Synovial joints share lots of common features but they can be classified according to their structure and the range of movement they allow.

The four main **joint classifications** are:

- pivot joint – seen at the atlas/axis at the top of the neck
- hinge joint – seen at the elbow, knee and ankle
- ball and socket joint – seen at the hip and shoulder
- condyloid joint – seen at the wrist.

> ## Key term
>
> **Classifications of joints:** There are four main classifications of joint: pivot joints, hinge joints, ball and socket joints and condyloid joints. Each type of joint has a specific range of movement.

## Activity

**4** **a)** Each of the sporting actions in the photos below relies on a specific classification of joint. For each sporting action, name the type of joint and describe what it is about the design of the joint that makes it capable of performing the action.

i

ii

iii

iv

v

vi

**b)** Could a hinge joint do the job of a ball and socket joint? Explain your answer.

# Movements possible at different joints

While most sporting actions require a combination of movements at a number of joints simultaneously, it is possible to isolate specific joint actions. The different movements at joints are named so that sporting actions can be described and analysed.

When looking at joints, those that can perform many different **movement types** are seen as having a large **range of movement**, while those restricted to a low number of movements are considered to have a low range of movement. For example, the knee (a hinge joint) has a limited range of movement because it can only flex and extend, whereas the hip (a ball and socket joint) has a far greater range of movement because it is capable of performing many different movements.

## Key terms

**Movement types:** Names used to identify directions of movement at joints. These include flexion, extension, adduction, abduction, rotation, circumduction, plantar-flexion and dorsi-flexion.

**Range of movement:** Different joints allow different movements to take place. Joints that can perform many different types of movements have a large range of movement.

## Exam tip

Movements are always described from the anatomical position, where a person is standing upright with their arms by the side of their body and their palms facing forwards. This links very closely with the information on planes and axes in chapter 2. See page 52.

## Flexion

The angle at a joint is decreased. Flexion can be seen as bending at a hinge joint and a condyloid joint, or when a limb moves in a forwards direction at a ball and socket joint.

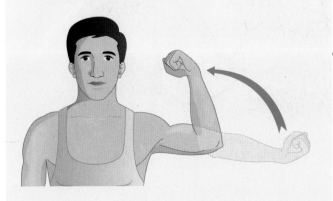

## Extension

The angle at a joint is increased. Extension can be seen as straightening at a hinge joint and a condyloid joint, or when a limb moves in a backwards direction at a ball and socket joint.

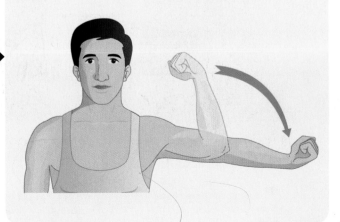

## Abduction

Abduction can be seen when a limb is moved away from the midline of the body at a ball and socket joint or a condyloid joint.

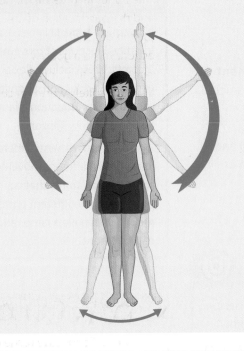

## Adduction

Adduction can be seen when a limb is brought back towards the midline of the body at a ball and socket joint or a condyloid joint.

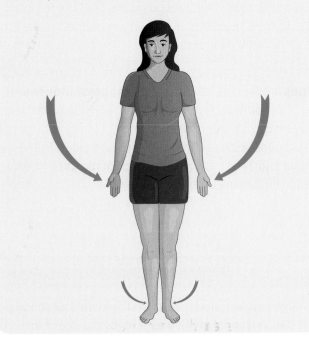

## Rotation

This is a twisting action where part of the body twists around its long axis at a pivot joint or at a ball and socket joint.

## Circumduction

This is a combination of flexion, abduction, adduction and extension and looks like you are drawing a circle in the air. This is possible at ball and socket joints and condyloid joints.

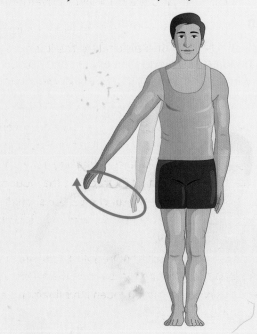

## Dorsi-flexion

Dorsi-flexion is only seen at the ankle – a hinge joint – when the toes are raised towards the shin.

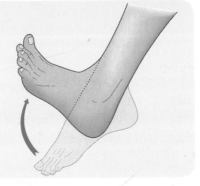

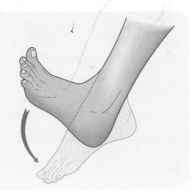

## Plantar-flexion

Plantar-flexion is only seen at the ankle, when the toes are pointed away from the shin.

## Ligaments and tendons

During movements, two connective tissues play a very important role at joints.

- **Ligaments** connect bone to bone and hold the joint together. They are tough and slightly elastic, so they help to prevent dislocations. A dislocation happens when a bone is forced out of place.

- **Tendons** connect muscles to bones, ensuring that when a muscle contracts, the effort is transferred to the bone and movement is created.

The tendons allow movement to happen, and the ligaments prevent the movement going too far and dislocating the joint.

### Key terms

**Ligament:** Connective tissue that attaches bone to bone at joints. Its role is to prevent dislocation.

**Tendon:** Connective tissue that attaches muscle to bone. Its role is to transfer the effort created by a contracting muscle to the bone, resulting in the movement of that bone.

## Activities

5   Provide a sporting example for each type of movement at each classification of joint where the movement is possible. For example: *Extension is seen at the elbow, which is a hinge joint, when making a chest pass in netball.*

6   Prepare a list of movement instructions that your partner can follow in order to perform a skill of your choice. You should start with them in the anatomical position. For example, you might start by telling your partner to "Flex your right elbow."

7   This squash player is using many joints. Explain, in your own words, the role that his ligaments and tendons play as he makes this movement. What would or would not happen if his ligaments and tendons did not do their jobs properly?

There are three main types of muscle within the body: **cardiac muscle**, **involuntary muscle** and **voluntary muscle**. All muscle is made up of fibres. It is the way that these fibres work which differentiates one type of muscle from another, and makes each type able to perform a specialist role.

## Cardiac muscle

Cardiac muscle is found exclusively in the heart. This type of muscle is not under our conscious control, and it contracts and relaxes continuously throughout our lives. Cardiac muscle provides the pumping action that circulates blood around the body. It responds to an internal electrical impulse and contracts, causing a heartbeat. These contractions drive blood around the body so that, amongst other things, oxygen can be delivered and waste products removed. This delivery and removal is the major role of the cardiac muscle when it comes to sport and physical activity. The beating of the heart (**heart rate**) and the strength with which it contracts (linked to **stroke volume**) alter in response to the intensity of activity.

> **Key terms**
>
> **Voluntary muscle:** Muscle involved in skeletal movement.
>
> **Involuntary muscle:** The muscle involved in digestion and vascular shunting.
>
> **Cardiac muscle:** The muscle of the heart, which pumps blood around the body.

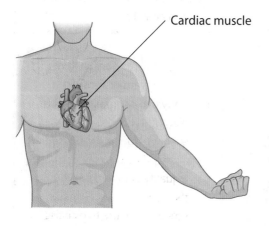

Cardiac muscle

◀ When swimming, cardiac muscle is responsible for the heart's pumping action, which delivers oxygen and nutrients in the blood to the working muscles.

## Involuntary muscle

Involuntary muscle is located through the middle layer of blood vessels and throughout the digestive system. Involuntary muscle is often referred to as smooth muscle. Like cardiac muscle, involuntary muscle operates without our conscious control. It has many roles, including digesting food and expelling waste from the body. Crucial to sport and physical activity is the role that it plays in the redistribution of blood, a process known as **vascular shunting**. Involuntary muscle controls the internal diameter – or "lumen" – of blood vessels. Through **vasodilation** (widening of the lumen) and **vasoconstriction** (narrowing of the lumen) of certain arteries, blood flow to active areas of the body increases while blood flow to inactive areas decreases. Blood is directed to where it is most needed: during exercise blood is directed towards the voluntary muscles used for movement.

> **Key terms**
>
> **Heart rate (HR):** The number of heart beats per minute, measured in beats per minute (bpm). For more information see page 38.
>
> **Stroke volume (SV):** The amount of blood pumped out of the heart per beat, measured in millilitres per heartbeat (ml/beat). For more information see page 38.

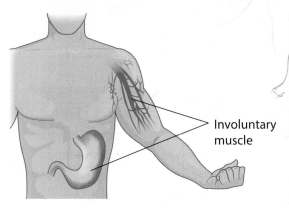

Involuntary muscle

▲ During badminton, involuntary muscle is responsible for vascular shunting, which allows oxygenated blood to be directed towards working muscles.

## Voluntary muscle

Voluntary muscles attach to your bones via tendons. Examples include the biceps and the triceps muscles. These muscles are under conscious control; you can decide when and how powerfully you contract them. Whether you are walking, running, throwing or kicking, voluntary muscles are crucial to creating movement. Even when you are sitting, many voluntary muscles are contracting to maintain your posture. As a result, voluntary muscles are crucial in all sporting and physical activity movements.

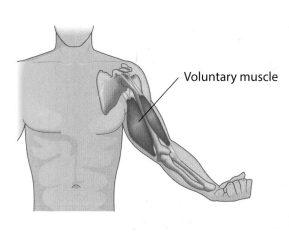

Voluntary muscle

▲ When playing football, voluntary muscles are crucial in allowing a person to move. Here we see a player running, which is a movement that requires many voluntary muscles.

## Exam tip

Make sure that you can link the characteristics of each muscle type with their role in sport and physical activity.

## Activity

8  Copy and complete this Venn diagram. List the qualities of each type of muscle in the appropriate circle. If they share a quality with another muscle, then write that quality in the space where the two circles overlap. If all three muscle types share a quality, then it should be written in the very centre. You may need to do some additional research.

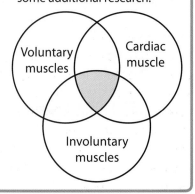

Voluntary muscles

Cardiac muscle

Involuntary muscles

# Voluntary muscles and their role in physical activity

Movement, sporting or otherwise, is produced when voluntary muscles, attached to bones by tendons, **contract** and the skeletal and muscular systems work together to produce movements. Sporting actions are strong examples of the work that the **musculo-skeletal system** does. A contracting voluntary muscle pulls on a bone, which alters the angle at a joint, and movement is produced.

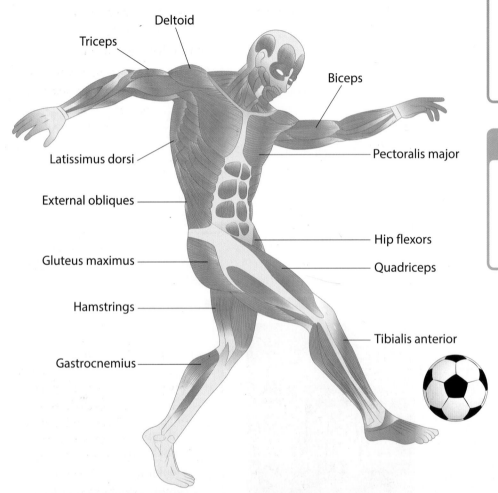

Deltoid
Triceps
Biceps
Latissimus dorsi
Pectoralis major
External obliques
Gluteus maximus
Hip flexors
Quadriceps
Hamstrings
Tibialis anterior
Gastrocnemius

## Key terms

**Contraction:** A muscle contracts when it is activated and tension is created. Muscles shorten and pull when they contract; they don't push.

**Musculo-skeletal system:** The name given to the combined body system that involves your muscles and your skeleton.

## Exam tip

You will be required to link specific muscles with specific movements. For example, *When the triceps muscle contracts it causes extension at the elbow, which is a hinge joint.*

## Activity

**9** Investigate the movements that are created when each of the voluntary muscles in the diagram contract. You'll probably need to get up and move about in order to work them all out. Copy and complete the table to record your findings.

| When this muscle contracts... | ...it causes this movement... | ...of this body part |
| --- | --- | --- |
| *When the tibialis anterior contracts* | *it causes dorsi-flexion* | *at the ankle.* |

Remember that muscles shorten and pull when they contract; they don't push.

# 1.7 Antagonistic pairs

Because muscles can only pull and are not capable of pushing, they are arranged in pairs on either side of joints. Movement is produced when one muscle contracts and pulls on a bone, while the opposite muscle relaxes and allows the bone to be pulled. The same process happens in the other direction when the other muscle contracts.

A pair of muscles is called an **antagonistic pair**. The muscle contracting is known as the **agonist**, while the opposite muscle, which is relaxing, is known as the **antagonist**.

## Key terms

**Antagonistic muscle pair:** A pair of muscles that work together to produce movement.

**Agonist:** The muscle within the pair that, at a given time, is contracting to pull on the bone and produce movement.

**Antagonist:** The muscle within the pair that, at a given time, is relaxing to allow movement to occur.

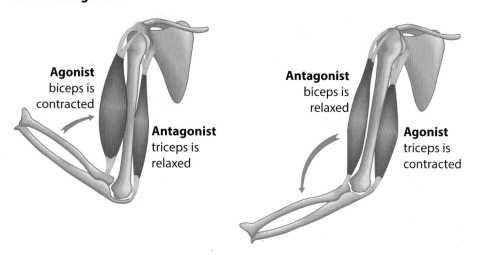

**Agonist**
biceps is contracted

**Antagonist**
triceps is relaxed

**Antagonist**
biceps is relaxed

**Agonist**
triceps is contracted

▲ The biceps and triceps contract and relax to allow the arm to flex and extend at the elbow.

◀ Look at this player. He is about to perform a volleyball set. Currently, his elbow joints are slightly flexed. As he executes the set, he needs to extend at the elbows quickly. To do this, the triceps will act as the agonist and contract to pull on the radius and ulna in the forearm. At the same time, the biceps will act as the antagonist and relax. This will allow the bones to be pulled. The biceps and triceps are working as an antagonistic pair. Extension at the elbow will take place, and the player's arms will straighten to produce the set shot.

## Activity

**10 a)** Model the action of the volleyball set and think about your triceps acting as the agonist as your arms extend at the elbow.

**b)** Place one hand around the inside of your opposite upper arm. Now imagine you have something heavy in your free hand, while you perform a biceps curl. As you go through the upward phase, you should feel your biceps getting bigger as it contracts as the agonist, causing flexion at the elbow. You should also feel the triceps getting longer and thinner as it relaxes as the antagonist. Describe what happens when you go through the downward phase of the movement.

**c)** Carry out a similar practical experiment and describe what happens when you flex and extend your knee.

The following muscles make up obvious antagonistic pairs:

- biceps and triceps, acting at the elbow to create flexion and extension

- hip flexor and gluteus maximus, acting at the hip to create flexion and extension

- hamstrings and quadriceps, acting at the knee to create flexion and extension

- tibialis anterior and gastrocnemius, acting at the ankle to create dorsi-flexion and plantar-flexion.

During sporting situations, antagonistic pairs swap roles continuously. A muscle acts as both an agonist and an antagonist depending on the movement required.

## Exam tip

If you remember these muscles in pairs, then you'll be able to provide excellent examples of antagonistic pairs.

◀ Look at this skier. As he flexes and extends at the hips – to crouch into turns and then stand up again – his hip flexors and gluteus maximus will switch between acting as the agonist and the antagonist.

# 1.8 Fast and slow twitch muscle fibre types

There are three types of muscle fibre:

- **type I:** slow twitch muscle fibres
- **type IIa:** fast twitch muscle fibres
- **type IIx:** fast twitch (very fast) muscle fibres.

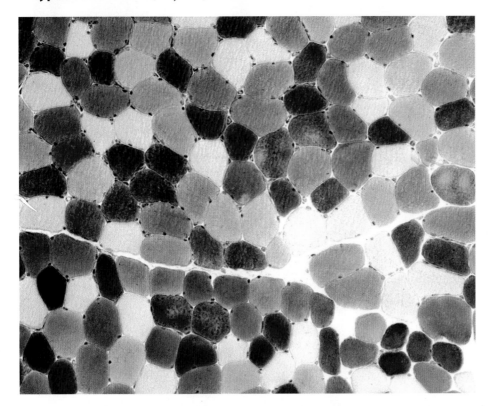

▲ We can see the different types of muscle fibre under a microscope. Type I muscle fibres are deep red, type IIa muscle fibres are pink and type IIx muscle fibres are white. This person has a fairly even balance of fibre types.

Every voluntary muscle in the body contains thousands of muscle fibres. The percentage of each type of muscle fibre that a person has, determines how effectively their muscles can perform in a particular activity. While some fibres can contract repeatedly over a long period, others can contract powerfully but only for a limited period before they require a rest.

In the same way that some people have blue eyes and some people have brown eyes, the make up of your voluntary muscles is genetic. Most of the population will have an even balance of all three types of muscle fibre. However, individuals who have a high percentage of a particular type are genetically advantaged towards particular activities. While training can develop the abilities of different fibres, it cannot change one type of muscle fibre into another type of muscle fibre.

## Key terms

**Type I muscle fibres:** These are also known as slow twitch muscle fibres. Type I muscle fibres are suited to low intensity aerobic work such as marathon running because they can be used for a long time without fatiguing.

**Type IIa muscle fibres:** These are fast twitch fibres. They are suited to lengthy anaerobic work, such as an 800 m race, and can be improved through endurance training to increase their resistance to fatigue.

**Type IIx muscle fibres:** These are fast twitch muscle fibres. They are used in anaerobic work and can generate much greater force than the other muscle fibre types, but they fatigue quickly. They are beneficial to 100 m sprinters. In the past, this type of muscle fibre has been referred to as "type IIb".

## Exam tip

Remember, fibre types are genetic. You have what you have. You can train them, but you can't change them.

## Type I muscle fibres

Slow twitch muscle fibres are designed to work aerobically as they are excellent at using oxygen to help create energy. They are very well suited to endurance events such as the 10,000 m and marathon as they do not fatigue quickly and can keep working for a long time. Compared to the other types of muscle fibre, they are not very powerful and contract relatively slowly. This means they are not well suited to high intensity activities.

**Summary:** Work aerobically, use oxygen. Linked to low intensity activity.

**Positives:** High aerobic capacity, high fatigue resistance.

**Negatives:** Low speed and force of contraction, low anaerobic capacity.

**Sporting example:** Long-distance running (10,000 m and marathon).

▲ Tirunesh Dibaba

## Type IIa muscle fibres

Type IIa fast twitch muscle fibres are designed to work anaerobically. They contract quickly with high force, but are able to work for a relatively long time. This means they are well suited to dynamic and relatively fast-paced activities lasting 30 seconds to two minutes, such as the 800 m and sections of invasion games requiring quick and powerful movements.

**Summary:** Work anaerobically. Linked to extended, high-intensity activity.

**Positives:** High speed and force of contraction, good strength and speed endurance.

**Negatives:** Not as fatigue-resistant as type I muscle fibres, and not as powerful as type IIx muscle fibres.

**Sporting examples:** 800 m runners, central-field invasion game players.

▲ David Rudisha

## Type IIx muscle fibres

These are pure, fast twitch muscle fibres, which work anaerobically. They contract very quickly and with huge force. They are explosive fibres with the potential for massive power output, and this suits short, high-intensity bursts of activity such as the 100 m event. They fatigue very quickly and cannot be used for long as they build lactic acid rapidly.

**Summary:** Work anaerobically. Linked to very high-intensity activity.

**Positives:** Very high speed and force of contraction, very high anaerobic capacity.

**Negatives:** Very low aerobic capacity, very low fatigue resistance.

**Sporting example:** 100 m sprinter.

▲ Dina Asher Smith

## Activities

11 Draw three boxes and fill them with small circles, like the ones in the picture of muscle fibres under a microscope on page 19. Label the boxes "Marathon runner", "800 m runner" and "Sprinter". Now colour in the circles to show how the muscles of an elite performer in those activities would look under a microscope. Remember, no one has 100% of any one fibre type.

12 In groups of three, decide who is going to represent type I muscle fibres, who is going to represent type IIa muscle fibres, and who is going to represent type IIx muscle fibres. Hold a debate about which of you has the greatest sporting potential and why you should be considered the most desirable type of muscle fibre. Give factual evidence to support your argument.

The **cardiovascular system** is made up of the heart, three types of blood vessel and the blood itself. The heart generates the pumping action, the vessels provide a circulatory network, and the blood itself acts as a carrier for blood cells, gases and nutrients.

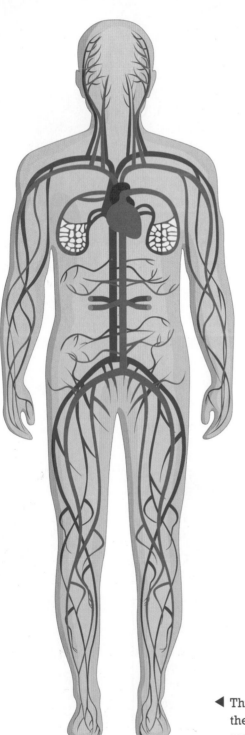

◀ This diagram shows the heart and the network of blood vessels that make up the cardiovascular system.

## Key terms

**Cardiovascular system:** the heart, blood vessels and blood.

**Functions of the cardiovascular system:** The three functions of the cardiovascular system are: transport, clotting and temperature regulation.

## Exam tip

Think of the cardiovascular system as a taxi company. The heart is the taxi rank, the point at which all the journeys start and where the taxis return afterwards. The blood vessels are the roads along which taxi journeys are made. The blood is the taxis themselves, carrying important items where they need to go before returning to the taxi rank.

It is the responsibility of the cardiovascular system to circulate blood all around the body and, in doing this, it serves three main functions.

## Transport

By acting as a carrier of oxygen and nutrients (such as glucose), blood delivers what the body needs to work. It also carries away waste products, such as carbon dioxide and lactic acid. This is crucial during physical activity, because the requirements for oxygen and nutrients go up when a person is exercising. The need to transport carbon dioxide and lactic acid away from the muscles also increases.

### Functions of the cardiovascular system

## Activity

**13** Write a short but memorable poem or limerick to help you recall the functions of the cardiovascular system.

## Clotting

Platelets in the blood form clots, which seal open wounds quickly. This process is important in guarding the body against infection and excessive bleeding. During many physical activities, the risk of a cut is increased and, therefore, clotting is important in ensuring that such injuries are not life threatening.

## Temperature regulation

By controlling the internal diameter (lumen) of blood vessels, the body is able to maintain its temperature fairly effectively at around 37 °C. When the body is too hot, vasodilation takes place, increasing blood flow to the skin where it is cooled. During physical activity the body generates more heat and it is, therefore, important to regulate temperature so that a person doesn't overheat. Overheating can lead to headaches, confusion and even loss of consciousness.

The heart pumps blood to two destinations simultaneously:

- to the lungs, where it becomes oxygenated before returning to the heart
- to the rest of the body, where is becomes deoxygenated as it delivers the oxygen it carries to the muscles and organs.

## The structure of the heart

The heart is made up of four chambers. The top two are called **atria** and the bottom two are called **ventricles**. Blood flow through them is guided by one-way valves. The left side of the heart deals with **oxygenated blood** (shown in red in the diagrams) and the right side of the heart accepts and pumps out **deoxygenated blood** (shown in blue on the diagrams).

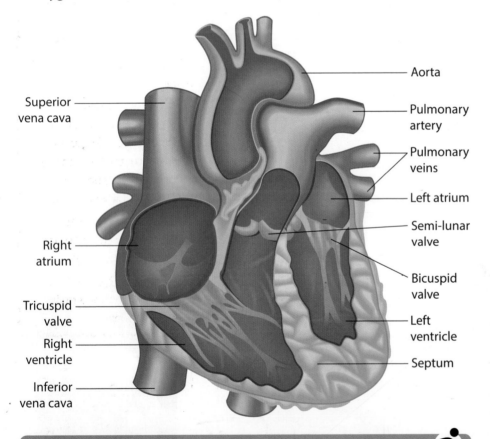

Superior vena cava

Right atrium

Tricuspid valve

Right ventricle

Inferior vena cava

Aorta

Pulmonary artery

Pulmonary veins

Left atrium

Semi-lunar valve

Bicuspid valve

Left ventricle

Septum

### Key terms

**Atria:** This is the plural of "atrium". There are two atria in the heart. These are the upper chambers of the heart where blood enters.

**Ventricles:** There are two ventricles in the heart. These are the lower chambers of the heart from where blood exits.

**Oxygenated blood:** Blood containing a high concentration of oxygen.

**Deoxygenated blood:** Blood containing a low concentration of oxygen.

### Activity

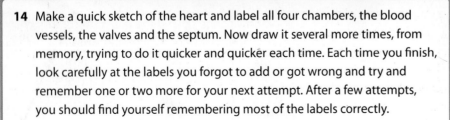

14 Make a quick sketch of the heart and label all four chambers, the blood vessels, the valves and the septum. Now draw it several more times, from memory, trying to do it quicker and quicker each time. Each time you finish, look carefully at the labels you forgot to add or got wrong and try and remember one or two more for your next attempt. After a few attempts, you should find yourself remembering most of the labels correctly.

### Exam tip

The heart is drawn as if you are looking down at in on a table, but it is labelled as if the heart is in your body. The heart's left-hand side is labelled "left" not the side that you see on the left when you are looking at the diagram. As a result, the labels appear to be the wrong way around; but they're not.

Because the heart beats in a very specific way and contains one-way valves, blood moves through the heart is a very regimented way.

> Blood returns from the body through the **superior vena cava** and the **inferior vena cava**.

↓

> Deoxygenated blood enters the right atrium.

↓

> Deoxygenated blood passes through the **tricuspid valve** into the right ventricle.

↓

> Deoxygenated blood is pumped through **pulmonary arteries** to the lungs. The **semi-lunar valves** prevent blood re-entering the heart.

↓

> *Blood is oxygenated at the lungs.*

↓

> Oxygenated blood returns to the heart through the **pulmonary veins.**

↓

> Oxygenated blood enters the left atrium of the heart.

↓

> Oxygenated blood passes through the **bicuspid valve** and into the left ventricle.

↓

> Oxygenated blood is pumped through the **aorta** to the muscles and organs of the body. The semi-lunar valves prevent blood re-entering the heart.

## Key terms

**Tricuspid valve:** A one-way gate that separates the right atrium from the right ventricle.

**Bicuspid valve:** A one-way gate that separates the left atrium from the left ventricle.

**Semi-lunar valves:** One-way gates at the entrance to the aorta and pulmonary artery, which prevent the backflow of the blood into the heart.

**Aorta:** The artery that carries blood from the heart to the rest of the body.

**Vena cava:** The large vein entering the right atrium of the heart that carries deoxygenated blood back from the body to the heart. There is an inferior vena cava and a superior vena cava.

**Pulmonary artery:** The artery that carries deoxygenated blood from the heart to the lungs.

**Pulmonary vein:** The vein that carries oxygenated blood from the lungs to the heart.

## Activity

**15** As a class, find a big space and create a huge diagram of the heart using cones. Make sure your heart has outer walls and all the blood vessels and valves are in place. Walk through the diagram in small groups, starting at the point where the vena cava enters the heart, describing your route as you take it. Take this book with you to check that the details are correct. If a group gets stuck, try giving them clues about what comes next.

## Exam tip

The volumes of blood that the heart pumps out, and how blood circulation is affected by exercise are covered on pages 38–9.

# Blood vessels and their role in physical activity

Having been pumped from the heart, blood travels around the body in blood vessels. There are three types of blood vessel, each with slightly different structural features. The reason for this difference is that each type of vessel carries blood at a different point in its journey and under different circumstances.

## Arteries

- **Arteries** carry blood away from the heart.

- Arteries carry oxygenated blood. The exception is the pulmonary artery, which carries deoxygenated blood.

- Blood pressure is high in the arteries and gets higher when exercise takes place.

- The blood travels at high speed in the arteries.

- The arteries have thick muscular walls and small **lumens**.

- The involuntary muscle in the walls of arteries is always under slight tension.

- When blood moves through arteries, it makes them pulse. As they retract to their normal diameter, blood is pushed along.

- During exercise, the arteries to active muscles dilate. This means that they increase in diameter, allowing more oxygenated blood to be carried to working muscles.

- During exercise, the arteries to inactive muscles and organs constrict. This means that they reduce in diameter and less blood is carried to inactive areas of the body.

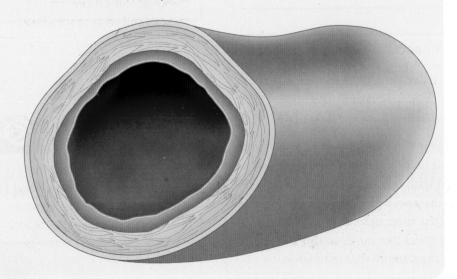

### Key terms

**Arteries:** Blood vessels that carry oxygenated blood from the heart to muscles and organs.

**Lumen:** The internal diameter of a blood vessel.

### Exam tip

Vasodilation and vasoconstriction are part of a process called vascular shunting, which takes place during exercise to direct blood to working muscles. This is explained on pages 42–3.

## Capillaries

- **Capillaries** look like a mesh wrapped around muscles and organs.

- There are lots of capillaries in every mesh.

- Each single capillary is very narrow. Blood cells have to travel through one at a time. This slows blood down.

- Each capillary has walls that are only one cell thick.

- Gases can diffuse through the walls of capillaries. Oxygen diffuses into muscles and organs through the capillaries. Carbon dioxide also diffuses into the blood through the capillaries. (See page 32 for more about diffusion.)

- Blood becomes deoxygenated at the capillaries.

- Capillaries are key during physical activity because they allow oxygen to enter the muscles through diffusion. Deoxygenated blood becomes oxygenated at the capillaries.

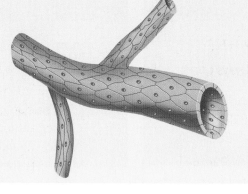

## Veins

- **Veins** carry blood back to the heart.

- Veins carry deoxygenated blood. The exception is the pulmonary vein, which carries oxygenated blood.

- Blood pressure is low in the veins.

- Blood travels at a fairly low speed in the veins.

- To prevent blood going in the wrong direction, veins have many one-way pocket valves.

- Veins have thinner walls than arteries.

- Veins have a larger lumen than arteries.

## Exam tip

During exercise more blood diffuses as it passes through the capillaries. This is explained in more detail on pages 42–3.

## Key term

**Capillaries:** Blood vessels that wrap around muscles and organs so that gaseous exchange can take place.

## Key term

**Veins:** Blood vessels that carry deoxygenated blood from muscles and organs to the heart.

## Activity

16 Model each of the three types of blood vessel in coloured modelling clay, paying particular attention to the unique features of each vessel.

# Blood and its role in physical activity

Blood contains four components, which are important for a healthy body and play a role in ensuring that a person can take part in physical activity and sport.

## Red blood cells

**Red blood cells** contain haemoglobin, a substance that allows oxygen to bind and be carried. As a result, red blood cells are responsible for oxygen transport. They are, therefore, key to all sports and physical activities that require any level of aerobic work, because they ensure that muscles have the oxygen they need to perform effectively. Activities that are most impacted by the work of red blood cells are endurance events like marathons and long-distance cycling.

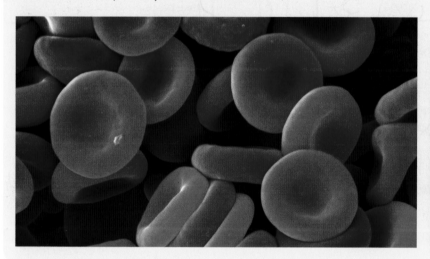

## White blood cells

**White blood cells** are part of the immune system. They travel in blood and fight disease and infection. They are, therefore, responsible for keeping athletes healthy, ensuring a sportsperson can train and compete.

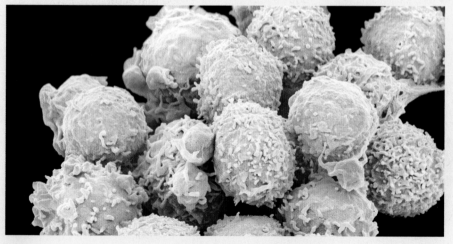

## Platelets

**Platelets** clot blood and scab around the site of an injury to seal open wounds. This is crucial to stop excessive bleeding and to heal the body quickly in order to prevent infection. This is important for a sports performer as it will stop injuries becoming life threatening.

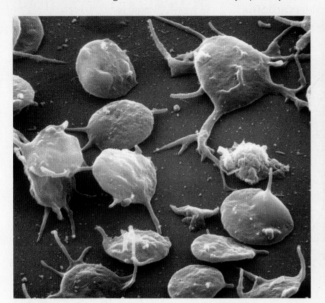

## Plasma

**Plasma** is the watery fluid part of blood that makes it a liquid. Without plasma, blood would not flow, and would, therefore, not be able to travel around the body.

## Exam tip

Information about the components of blood links closely to information about the functions of the cardiovascular system (pages 22–3). And without the heart pumping the blood around the body (pages 24–5) and the blood vessels providing the network for it to travel in (pages 26–7), the blood alone would be useless. Make sure you link all the information about the cardiovascular system together.

## Activity

**17** Create a comic strip with one of the four components of blood as a superhero. Demonstrate, through pictures and text, what the role of the superhero cell is and how it performs its duties. Be sure to have the superhero cell being super in a sporting context.

The respiratory system has two roles. Firstly, it brings oxygen into the body, so that it can help to produce energy aerobically. Secondly, it expels carbon dioxide, a waste product that is created in the muscles when we exercise.

▶ **This diagram shows the main components of the respiratory system.**

## Key terms

**Inhale:** We inhale air when we breathe in. The process of inhaling is called "inhalation".

**Exhale:** We exhale air when we breathe out. The process of exhaling is called "exhalation".

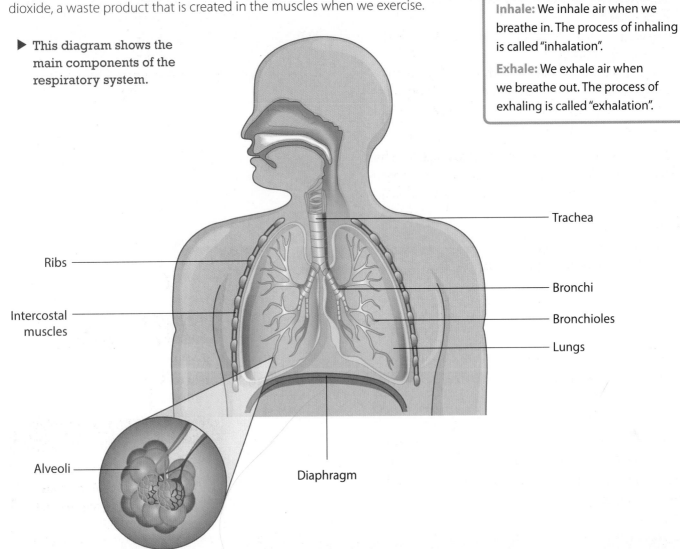

Trachea

Ribs

Bronchi

Intercostal muscles

Bronchioles

Lungs

Alveoli

Diaphragm

## The composition of the air that we breathe

It is important to note that the air we breathe in (or **inhale**) and the air that we breathe out (or **exhale**) is the same air; it is simply the gas content of that air that changes while it is in our lungs.

We can see by looking at these two pie charts that there is more oxygen in inhaled air than there is in exhaled air. We can also see that there is more carbon dioxide in the air we breathe out.

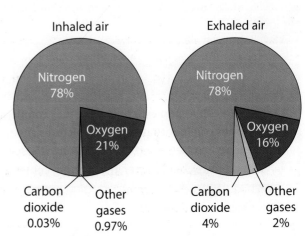

Inhaled air

Nitrogen 78%

Oxygen 21%

Carbon dioxide 0.03%

Other gases 0.97%

Exhaled air

Nitrogen 78%

Oxygen 16%

Carbon dioxide 4%

Other gases 2%

# The mechanics of breathing

## Inhalation

1. The diaphragm and intercostal muscles contract.
2. The diaphragm flattens and pulls the bottom of the lungs down.
3. The intercostal muscles pull the ribs and, therefore, the lungs outwards.
4. The lungs increase in size and the air pressure inside the lungs is reduced.
5. The air pressure outside the body is now higher than the air pressure inside the body. Air travels from areas of high pressure to areas of low pressure, and so air is pulled into the lungs.

During exercise, extra muscles are used to make the chest cavity even bigger, to pull even more air in. This is because the working muscles need more oxygen during exercise.

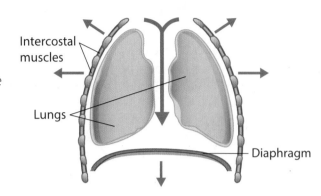

## Exhalation

1. The diaphragm and intercostal muscles relax.
2. The diaphragm moves back up into a dome shape.
3. The relaxed intercostal muscles allow the ribs and lungs to move inwards.
4. The lungs reduce in size and the air pressure inside the lungs is increased.
5. The air pressure outside the body is now lower than the air pressure inside the body. Air travels from areas of high pressure to areas of low pressure so air leaves the lungs.

During exercise, extra muscles are used to force air out, which allows you to breath more frequently and more deeply. This is because more carbon dioxide is created and it needs to be exhaled.

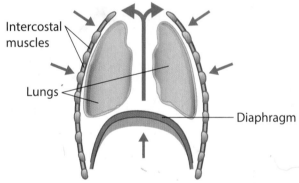

> ## Exam tip
>
> The volumes of air that are inhaled and exhaled, and how these are affected by exercise, are covered on pages 40–1.

> ## Activities
>
> **18** Look at the pie charts showing the composition of air on the opposite page. Can you explain why there is a difference in the composition of air we inhale and the composition of air that we exhale? Also, what can you interpret and explain about the levels of nitrogen in each pie chart?
>
> **19** Write a list of the key phrases used to describe the functioning of the respiratory system. Find an animation on the Internet of lungs inflating and deflating as a person inhales and exhales. Describe what is happening as you watch the animation, using all the phrases that you have written down. It might be useful to record this onto your phone, so that you can listen to it again when you are revising.

> ## Exam tip
>
> It is a common misunderstanding that the lungs work like a balloon. They do not. With a balloon, the air being blown in makes the balloon get bigger. The air pushes out the sides of the balloon. With the lungs, muscles actively change the size of the chest cavity, which stretches the lungs and pulls air in.

# Gaseous exchange

Once the alveoli in the lungs have filled with air, a process known as **gaseous exchange** takes place. Oxygen moves from the air in the alveoli into the blood in the capillaries, while carbon dioxide moves from the blood in the capillaries into the air in the alveoli.

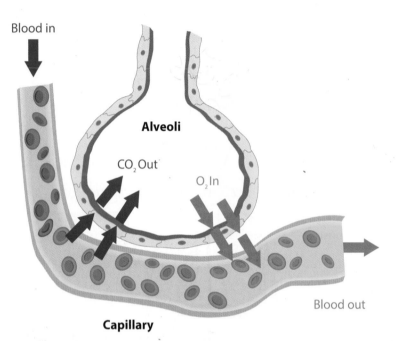

Blood in

Alveoli

$CO_2$ Out

$O_2$ In

Blood out

**Capillary**

▲ This basic diagram shows how oxygen ($O_2$) and carbon dioxide ($CO_2$) exchange with one another in the alveoli.

## Diffusion

In order to understand gaseous exchange, you need to understand the process of **diffusion**. This is the term used to describe how molecules move from an area of higher concentration to an area of lower concentration in an attempt to reach a balance. After you have inhaled:

- there is a higher concentration of oxygen in the air in the alveoli than there is in the blood and, as a result, oxygen molecules diffuse into the blood in the capillaries

- there is a higher concentration of carbon dioxide in the blood in the capillaries than there is in the air in the alveoli and, as a result, carbon dioxide molecules diffuse from the blood in the capillaries into the air in the alveoli.

Gaseous exchange is the diffusion of gases in opposite directions at the same time. This means that oxygen diffuses into the blood in the capillaries at the same time as carbon dioxide diffuses into the air in the alveoli.

The alveoli are perfectly designed for diffusion, which allows the process of gaseous exchange to be very efficient.

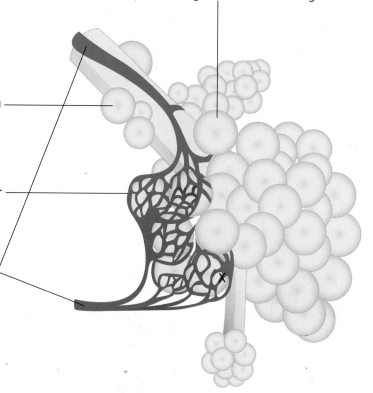

The alveoli have moist thin walls, which are perfect for gases to diffuse through

There are around 400 million alveoli in your lungs, providing a massive surface area for diffusion to take place

The capillaries and alveoli are very closely wrapped together so that gases only have to diffuse across a short distance

The blood supply to the alveoli is substantial so that lots of gas can be carried away quickly

## Gaseous exchange during exercise

During exercise, the muscles use more oxygen. As a result, the blood returning from the muscles has a lower than normal concentration of oxygen in it. Because the difference between the concentration of oxygen in the blood and in the air in the alveoli is greater, more oxygen diffuses into the blood.

At the same time, more carbon dioxide is created in the muscles during exercise. As a result of the higher concentration of carbon dioxide in the blood and a greater difference between this and the concentration of carbon dioxide in the air in the alveoli, more carbon dioxide is diffused into the air in the alveoli.

This means that a greater level of gaseous exchange takes place during exercise. The exact level of gaseous exchange depends on the intensity of the activity.

**Exam tip**

There are lots of animations available online that will allow you to see gaseous exchange happening as the fluid process that it is.

**Activity**

20 Create a video presentation, or a storyboard for a video presentation, on gaseous exchange that can be shown to a class of Key Stage 3 students. You'll need to consider the best way to present the information. What is the simplest way to help someone to understand it?

The cardiovascular and respiratory systems work together to supply muscles with a continuous supply of oxygen. They also work together to remove carbon dioxide. When someone is taking part in physical activity, they have to work harder because the demand for oxygen increases and there is more carbon dioxide to remove.

### Activity

21 Write two short-answer exam-style questions about how the cardiovascular and respiratory systems work together, along with the mark schemes for both questions. Use the flow diagram to help you. Swap your questions with a partner and test one another's knowledge.

Air is inhaled.

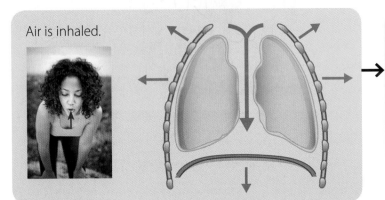

Air journeys though the respiratory system to the alveoli.

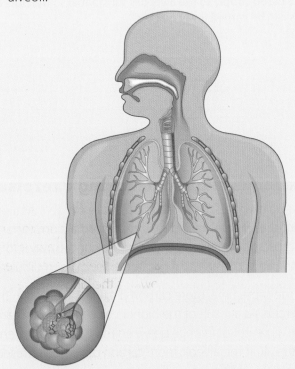

Air travels back though the respiratory system and is exhaled.

Gaseous exchange takes place at the alveoli. Carbon dioxide diffuses into the air.

Blood in

**Alveoli**

$CO_2$ Out

**Capillary**

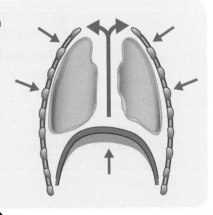

The pulmonary artery carries deoxygenated blood to the lungs.

Gaseous exchange takes place at the alveoli. Oxygen diffuses into the blood in the capillaries.

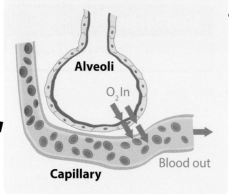

Oxygenated blood is carried from the lungs to the heart in the pulmonary vein.

Oxygenated blood enters the left atrium, moves through the bicuspid valve and into the left ventricle before being pumped towards the rest of the body via the aorta.

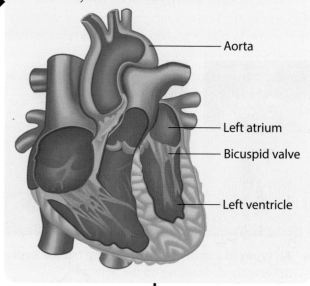

- Aorta
- Left atrium
- Bicuspid valve
- Left ventricle

The aorta carries oxygenated blood to other arteries.

The arteries carry oxygenated blood to the muscles and organs all over the body.

Oxygenated blood moves through the capillaries, where gaseous exchange takes place. Oxygen diffuses into the muscle or organ and carbon dioxide diffuses into the blood. The blood is now deoxygenated.

The veins carry the deoxygenated blood back to the heart.

Deoxygenated blood enters the right atrium through the superior vena cava and inferior vena cava. It moves through the tricuspid valve into the right ventricle, before being pumped towards the lungs via the pulmonary artery.

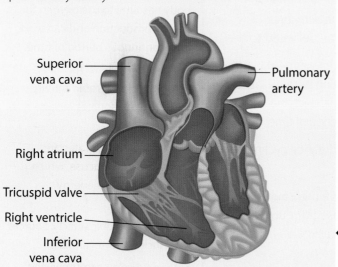

- Superior vena cava
- Pulmonary artery
- Right atrium
- Tricuspid valve
- Right ventricle
- Inferior vena cava

# 1.17 Aerobic and anaerobic exercise

Your body requires **energy** to work. Whether you are sitting in a chair with your muscles contracting to keep you upright, or sprinting 100 m with your muscles contracting to power you down the track, your muscles require energy.

▲ All types of activity require energy but the energy is produced differently depending on the activity.

There are two methods that your muscles can use to produce energy:

- Aerobically, using oxygen
- Anaerobically, without oxygen.

Both these methods are effective for producing energy and two factors determine which method is used:

- The **intensity** of the activity: how powerful it is.
- The **duration** of activity: how long the activity lasts for.

## Aerobic energy production
**Aerobic energy production takes place in the presence of oxygen.**

The body will be able to work aerobically if the intensity of the activity is moderate or lower. This is so that there is time for oxygen to be delivered to the working muscles, and processed, during the activity.

Producing energy aerobically is the body's preferred way of working because lots of energy can be produced this way and there are few harmful by-products created. Consequently, people working aerobically can work for a long period of time.

Examples of aerobic activities include marathon running, endurance cycling or long-distance, open-water swimming.

Aerobic energy production can use **carbohydrates** or **fat** as a fuel source. Carbon dioxide and water are by-products. The water is released through sweat, while the carbon dioxide is transported back to the lungs and exhaled.

carbohydrate → **glucose** + oxygen = ENERGY + carbon dioxide + water

fat → **fatty acids** + oxygen = ENERGY + carbon dioxide + water

## Anaerobic energy production

**Anaerobic energy production takes place without the presence of oxygen.**

When the intensity of an activity is high and muscular contractions need to be powerful and fast, oxygen cannot be processed quickly enough for the body to use it. As a result, the body produces energy anaerobically, without oxygen. This does not mean that you do not have to breathe. It simply means that your muscular contractions are happening too rapidly for oxygen to be delivered in time to be used.

While anaerobic energy can be produced quickly, it cannot be produced for a long duration. This is because **lactic acid** is a by-product of anaerobic energy production. As lactic acid builds up in muscles, they become fatigued and cannot function properly. Therefore, a person will need to rest before they can produce another burst of high-intensity anaerobic work so that their anaerobic energy system can recover.

Examples of anaerobic activities are events like the 100 m or 200 m sprint, or short sharp activities, like the high jump, that happen too quickly to allow oxygen to be used.

Anaerobic energy production uses carbohydrate as a fuel source.

carbohydrate → glucose = ENERGY + lactic acid

## Is an activity aerobic or anaerobic?

Any activity that goes go on for some time and where you have to think about "pacing yourself" will be largely aerobic. Activities where you go all out for a short period of time will be largely anaerobic. Games, like football, require a combination of aerobic and anaerobic energy production depending on the specific scenario taking place at the time. Sprinting up the wing is anaerobic, while holding position as a centre back is aerobic.

Intensity tops duration. If you walk across the room slowly for two seconds, the low intensity of the activity means it is aerobic regardless of the fact that you only did it for a short duration.

**Key terms**

**Anaerobic work:** Working at a high intensity without oxygen for energy production. The work period will be short in duration, because the energy is limited.

**Lactic acid:** A by-product of energy production, which is formed when the body is exercising anaerobically at high intensity. A build up of lactic acid results in muscle fatigue.

**Exam tip**

There is more about lactic acid and recovery on pages 44–5.

## Activities

**22 a)** Jog for a distance of about 1000 m at a moderate to low intensity. Stop and discuss how you feel. How was the energy used by your working muscles produced?

　**b)** Sprint as far as you can. (The furthest anyone will get will probably be 200 m.) What starts to happen in your legs the further you go? Can you explain this?

**23 a)** Write down a list of ten sporting activities and add the relative intensity and duration alongside each one.

　**b)** Place each sporting activity on a continuum, with the most aerobic at one end, and the most anaerobic at the other. You may need to debate the exact position of some in the middle. Remember that the intensity and duration of each activity are the two things to think about when considering where they should go on the continuum.

## Cardiac values and the cardiac equation

In order to understand the short-term effect of exercise on the heart and the cardiac changes that take place when a person exercises, we first need to look at the cardiac equation.

> The **cardiac equation:**
>
> stroke volume (SV) × heart rate (HR) = cardiac output (Q)

There are three cardiac values in the cardiac equation.

- **Stroke Volume (SV)** is the amount of blood pumped out of the heart per beat. The average resting stroke volume is around 70 millilitres per heart beat (ml/beat).

- **Heart rate (HR)** is the number of beats per minute that the heart generates. The average resting heart rate is around 75 beats per minute (bpm).

- **Cardiac output (Q)** is the volume of blood pumped out of the heart per minute. The average resting cardiac output is around 5 litres per minute (l/min).

The values in the cardiac equation alter when you exercise. They increase because the working muscles need more oxygen and so your blood needs to circulate around your body more quickly. Your heart, therefore, increases the amount of blood being pumped out per minute, which increases the speed at which your blood circulates. As a result, oxygen is delivered to your muscles more quickly to meet their demands and allow them to work aerobically, while the extra carbon dioxide created by your working muscles is carried away more quickly.

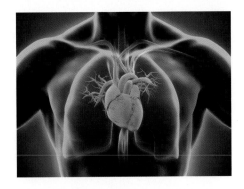

▲ "Cardiac" means related to the heart.

### Key terms

**Cardiac equation:** stroke volume × heart rate = cardiac output (SV × HR = Q)

**Cardiac output (Q):** The volume of blood pumped out of the heart per minute, measured in litres per minute (l/min).

### Exam tip

You will need to know about the cardiac equation when you study the long-term effects of exercise on pages 90–2. You will find out about, among other things, what resting heart rate and resting stroke volume tell us about fitness levels.

### Activities DATA

24  In a state of rest, find your pulse at either the carotid artery (in your neck) or the radial artery (in your wrist) and count how many times your heart beats in one minute. This is your resting heart rate in beats per minute.

25  **a)** Do you remember taking your resting heart rate? It is now time to generate more heart rate data of your own. Take part in some vigorous exercise, stopping periodically to take your heart rate. Record the information in a table before presenting it on a graph like the ones shown on page 39. Then interpret the graph. What does it tell you?

   **b)** Work with a partner to extend this activity and create different graphs. One of you could work continuously, which may allow you to see a plateau, while the other works in an interval style, which would show you how heart rate responds to exercise intensity.

   **c)** Compare your graphs with others. What do you learn from the analysis?

### Exam tip

You need to know how to interpret graphs showing responses to exercise. Note what is on the *x* and *y* axes, and the scale that each graph uses. Also, when a line on a graph flattens out, it is said to "reach a plateau".

## The short-term effect of exercise on stroke volume (SV)

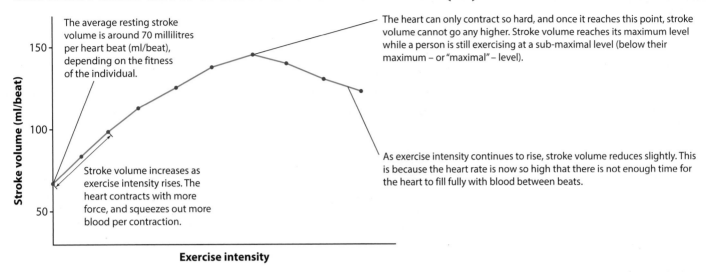

The average resting stroke volume is around 70 millilitres per heart beat (ml/beat), depending on the fitness of the individual.

The heart can only contract so hard, and once it reaches this point, stroke volume cannot go any higher. Stroke volume reaches its maximum level while a person is still exercising at a sub-maximal level (below their maximum – or "maximal" – level).

Stroke volume increases as exercise intensity rises. The heart contracts with more force, and squeezes out more blood per contraction.

As exercise intensity continues to rise, stroke volume reduces slightly. This is because the heart rate is now so high that there is not enough time for the heart to fill fully with blood between beats.

## The short-term effect of exercise on heart rate (HR)

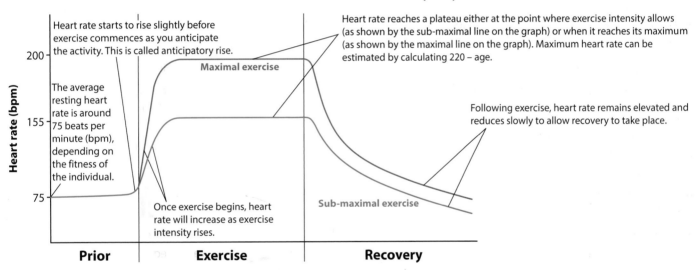

Heart rate starts to rise slightly before exercise commences as you anticipate the activity. This is called anticipatory rise.

The average resting heart rate is around 75 beats per minute (bpm), depending on the fitness of the individual.

Heart rate reaches a plateau either at the point where exercise intensity allows (as shown by the sub-maximal line on the graph) or when it reaches its maximum (as shown by the maximal line on the graph). Maximum heart rate can be estimated by calculating 220 – age.

Following exercise, heart rate remains elevated and reduces slowly to allow recovery to take place.

Once exercise begins, heart rate will increase as exercise intensity rises.

## The short-term effect of exercise on cardiac output (Q)

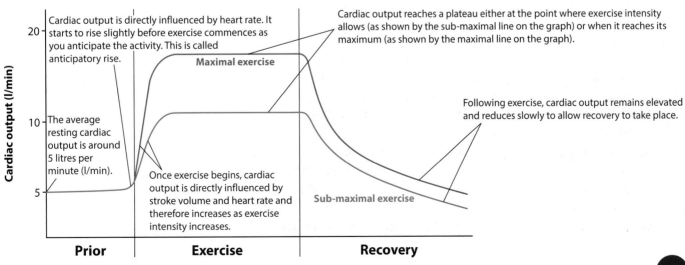

Cardiac output is directly influenced by heart rate. It starts to rise slightly before exercise commences as you anticipate the activity. This is called anticipatory rise.

The average resting cardiac output is around 5 litres per minute (l/min).

Cardiac output reaches a plateau either at the point where exercise intensity allows (as shown by the sub-maximal line on the graph) or when it reaches its maximum (as shown by the maximal line on the graph).

Following exercise, cardiac output remains elevated and reduces slowly to allow recovery to take place.

Once exercise begins, cardiac output is directly influenced by stroke volume and heart rate and therefore increases as exercise intensity increases.

# The short-term effects of exercise on the respiratory system

## Respiratory values and the respiratory equation

As with the short-term effects of exercise on the heart, in order to understand the short-term effects of exercise on the respiratory system, we first need to look at the respiratory equation.

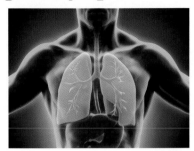

The **respiratory equation**:

tidal volume (TV) × frequency (f) = minute ventilation (VE)

There are four lung values that you need to be aware of:

- **Tidal volume (TV)** is the amount of air inhaled or exhaled per breath. This is your depth of breathing. Resting tidal volume is around 500 ml.

- **Frequency (f)** is the number of breaths taken per minute. This is your rate of breathing. Resting frequency is between 12 and 20 breaths.

- **Minute ventilation (VE)** is the amount of air inhaled or exhaled per minute.

- **Vital capacity** is the maximum amount of air exhaled following a maximum inhalation.

These four lung values can be measured using a spirometer. Lines moving upwards on a spirometer trace show inhalation, while lines going down show exhalation.

### Key terms

**Respiratory equation:** tidal volume × frequency = minute ventilation (TV × f = VE).

**Tidal volume (TV):** The amount of air inhaled or exhaled per breath, measured in millilitres (ml). It is also referred to as your "depth of breathing".

**Frequency (f):** The number of breaths taken per minute, measured in breaths. It is also referred to as your "rate of breathing".

**Minute ventilation:** The amount of air inhaled or exhaled per minute, measured in litres (l).

**Vital capacity:** The maximum amount of air exhaled following a maximum inhalation.

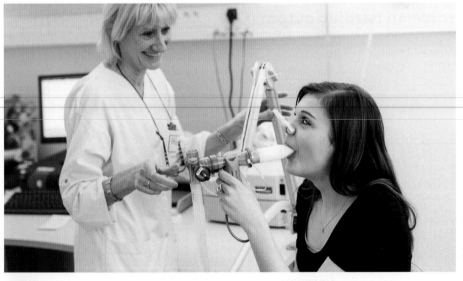

◀ A spirometer is a machine used to measure lung activity.

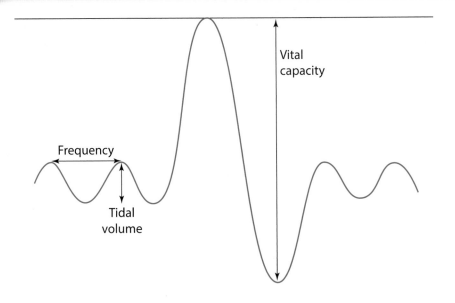

▲ Tidal volume, frequency and vital capacity are recorded on a spirometer trace, which is drawn by a spirometer.

## The short-term effect of exercise on the respiratory equation

When you exercise, your working muscles demand more oxygen. As a result, your lungs need to inhale more air. The frequency of your breathing and tidal volume increase. This allows more oxygen to diffuse into the blood stream and circulate around the body. In addition, when you exercise, your muscles create more carbon dioxide, which needs to be exhaled. An increase in the frequency of breathing and tidal volume allows this to happen.

### Activity

26 Copy the rest to exercise spirometer trace and annotate your diagram to explain why tidal volume and frequency change from rest to exercise. Include information on why this is so important for a sports performer.

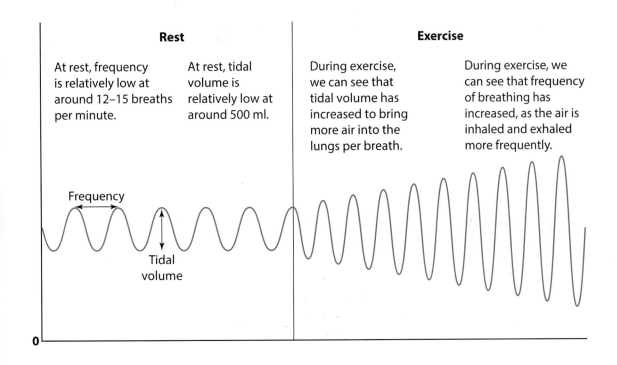

During exercise, it is not only important to breathe in more air and circulate oxygenated blood more quickly, it is also crucial to send the blood to the working muscles so the oxygen and other important nutrients are delivered to where they are needed most.

With stroke volume and heart rate increased, blood is able to reach the muscles quickly so long as it is redistributed in that direction.

### The redistribution of blood flow during physical activity

When exercise begins, the body alters its priorities. While at rest, a high proportion of blood is directed towards the organs, but during exercise the majority of blood is directed towards the voluntary muscles. For example, blood is directed away from the digestive system in favour of supplying the quadriceps and hamstrings. This ensures that the voluntary muscles are able to work aerobically, which is the most efficient way for them to work.

The process of redistributing blood when exercise begins is called **vascular shunting.** It is achieved by vasodilation and vasoconstriction, which is altering the size of the artery lumens supplying different areas of the body.

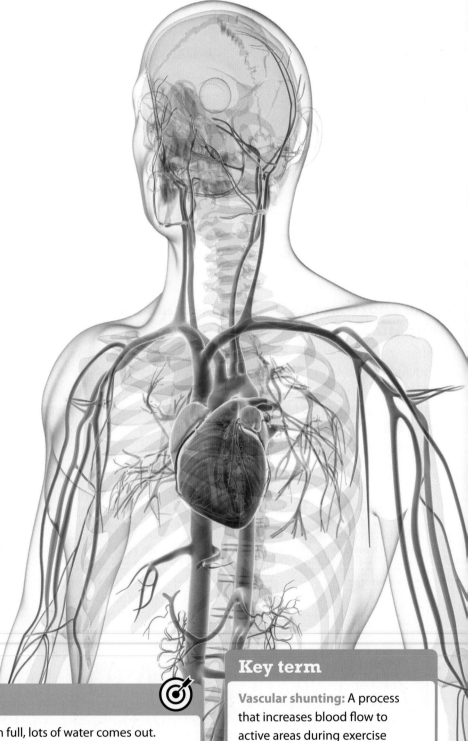

### Exam tip

Think of arteries like taps. If you turn a tap on full, lots of water comes out. When a tap is only partially turned on, a small amount of water comes out. Vascular shunting is like turning the taps to the organs off and turning the taps to the muscles on.

### Key term

**Vascular shunting:** A process that increases blood flow to active areas during exercise by diverting blood away from inactive areas. This is achieved by vasoconstriction and vasodilation.

## Vasoconstriction

**Vasoconstriction** is the narrowing of the internal diameter (lumen) of a blood vessel to restrict the volume of blood travelling through it. The arteries constrict during exercise so that less blood is delivered to inactive areas.

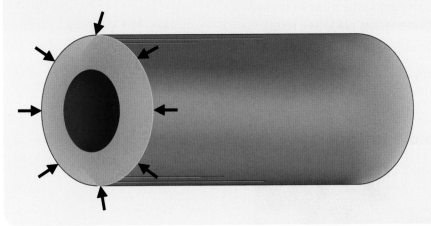

## Normal vascular tone

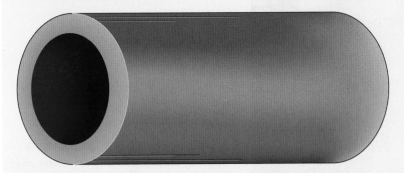

## Vasodilation

**Vasodilation** is the widening of the lumen of a blood vessel to increase the volume of blood travelling through it. The arteries dilate during exercise so that more blood is delivered to active areas, increasing their oxygen supply.

Without vascular shunting you would find taking part in sport unsustainable. Your muscles would be forced to work anaerobically and this would lead to early muscle fatigue.

### Key terms

**Vasoconstriction:** The narrowing of the internal diameter (lumen) of a blood vessel to decrease blood flow.

**Vasodilation:** The widening of the internal diameter (lumen) of a blood vessel to increase blood flow.

### Activity

27 Write down all the key phrases relating to vascular shunting on a piece of paper. Include "arteries", "vasoconstriction", "active areas" etc. Now attempt to explain the process to a partner without using any of these terms. You'll need to be very creative with your vocabulary! Once you've done that, write an explanation of vascular shunting using all the phrases and terms, which should be much easier.

During aerobic exercise, more oxygen diffuses into the working muscles from the blood. This is because the concentration of oxygen in the muscles is lower because they are working harder and more diffusion takes place as a result.

Muscles will work aerobically if the activity allows but if the activity is too intense, they will be forced to work anaerobically. Blood leaving the muscles will contain lower levels of oxygen and higher levels of carbon dioxide and lactic acid, if the muscles work anaerobically.

## Lactate accumulation and muscle fatigue

If the muscles are working aerobically, then lactic acid production will be low. However, if the activity being undertaken has anaerobic elements, which most do, then lactic acid will accumulate relatively quickly. Lactic acid is a by-product formed when the body is exercising anaerobically at high intensity. A build up of lactic acid results in muscle fatigue. **Muscle fatigue** is a reduction in the ability of a muscle to produce force.

◀ Muscle fatigue has an impact on a sportsperson, who experiences pain and reduced performance as a result.

## Activity

**DATA**

**28** Can you interpret the data plotted on this graph? This graph shows **lactate accumulation**.

*[Graph: y-axis labelled "Lactate", x-axis labelled "Heart rate". Curve remains low and flat then rises sharply at higher heart rate.]*

### Key term

**Muscle fatigue:** A reduction in a muscle's ability to produce force.

### Key term

**Lactate accumulation:** The name given to the process of lactic acid accumulating within the blood and muscles due to increased work intensity.

◀ When lactate levels get very high – often at the end of a game when a person has been regularly working anaerobically throughout – it can cause players real problems.

**Activity** 〈DATA〉

29 Collect, present and interpret heart rate recovery data:

a) Get yourself ready. Then raise your heart rate nice and high by taking part in some kind of vigorous activity for at least five minutes.

b) Collect your data. Measure your heart rate when it is really high by taking your pulse. Now take pulse measurements regularly as you recover. Measure it, wait 30 seconds, measure it again and so on. See how long it takes for your heart rate to return to resting level.

c) Plot your heart rate recovery data on a line graph. Label the *x* axis "Time", and the *y* axis "Heart rate (HR)".

d) Interpret your data. What does the data tell you about heart rate recovery?

## Recovery

An oxygen debt is created when muscles work anaerobically. This means that when you have finished exercising, and are in the recovery phase, your cardiovascular and respiratory systems continue to work hard to repay the debt and replenish your muscles with oxygen. Respiratory values stay high, cardiac values remain elevated, and blood continues to be directed towards the working muscles after exercise has stopped. These return to resting levels slowly as the body recovers.

◀ This runner is recovering and is taking lots of deep breaths; these breaths have a high frequency and a high tidal volume. The heart rate is elevated too, and this ensures that the muscles are replenished with oxygen.

# Exam-style questions

**1** Identify the structure labelled A in **Figure 1**. (1)

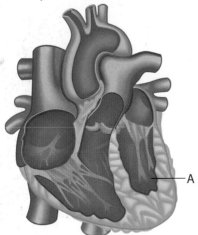

▲ **Figure 1**

**A** Aorta
**B** Left ventricle
**C** Left atrium
**D** Right ventricle

**2** Which one of the following are examples of short bones? (1)
**A** Carpals
**B** Phalanges
**C** Ribs
**D** Vertebrae

**3** Which one of the following movements is possible at a hinge joint? (1)
**A** Elevation
**B** Extension
**C** Rotation
**D** Circumduction

**4** Which one of the following is a feature of an artery? (1)
**A** Blood is carried at low pressure
**B** One cell thick
**C** Valves to prevent backflow
**D** Thick muscular wall

**5** Muscles are made up of different fibre types. Describe the characteristics of type IIx fibres that make them well suited to sprint events. (3)

**6** Muscles work with the skeleton to bring about specific movements. Complete **Table 1** by:
**a)** stating the function of each muscle
**b)** giving an example of a specific sporting movement that uses each muscle.

**Table 1**

| Muscle | a) Function | b) Specific sporting movement |
|---|---|---|
| Pectoralis major | (1) | (1) |
| Gastrocnemius | (1) | (1) |

**7** Describe one function of the cardiovascular system. (3)

**8** **Figure 2** shows an antagonistic pair of muscles being used to lift a weight.

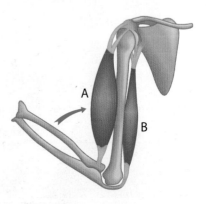

▲ **Figure 2**

Explain the role of the muscles marked in making this movement possible.
**A:** (2)
**B:** (2)

**9** Describe gaseous exchange and evaluate the extent to which it is important during a 100 m sprint and during a marathon. (9)

**10** Evaluate how the short-term effects of exercise can both benefit and limit performance in a rugby match. (9)

# 2 Movement analysis

When you have worked through this chapter, you will have developed knowledge and understanding of:

- first, second and third class levers and their use in physical activity

- mechanical advantage and disadvantage of the body's lever systems and the impact this has on sporting performance

- planes and axes of movement applied to sporting actions.

**Levers** are seen in everyday life as well as in sport and exercise. A lever system is a rigid bar that moves around a fixed fulcrum with two forces applied to it. Levers can change the size or direction of the effort used to make a task more manageable.

All levers consist of three key elements:

1 **Fulcrum:** a fixed pivot point.
2 **Effort:** the source of the energy that will do the work.
3 **Load:** the weight/resistance to be moved.

## Activity

1

The picture shows how a lever can be useful.
a) Explain how this lever works and what advantage a person gains using a lever in this situation.
b) Can you identify the fulcrum, effort and load in the picture?

## First, second and third class levers

There are three **classes of lever**: first class levers, second class levers and third class levers. The positioning of the fulcrum, load and effort in relation to each other will determine what class the lever is.

In the human body, the musculo-skeletal system creates levers around every joint. These allow us to move. The joint acts as the fulcrum, effort comes from contracting muscles and the load is the body part being moved, plus any additional objects held or resistance met. The body contains all classes of lever, but third class levers are most common.

## Key terms

**Lever:** A rigid bar or object that moves around a fixed fulcrum with two forces applied to it.

**Fulcrum:** A fixed pivot point. For example, a joint in the body.

**Effort:** The source of the energy. For example, muscles in the body.

**Load:** The weight/resistance to be moved. For example, a body part plus anything held or resistance met.

## Key term

**Class of lever:** The type of lever. There are first class, second class and third class levers.

## Exam tip

You will be expected to draw and label simple lever set-ups, so you'll need a method for remembering the difference between first, second and third class levers.

Try imagining: one see-saw, two wheelbarrows and three fishing rods.

Or use the mnemonic "1, 2, 3, F, L, E" to help you remember the middle element of each class of lever.

| Class of lever | Lever drawing | Well-known example for you to remember easily | Best example in the human body |
|---|---|---|---|
| **First class lever** | 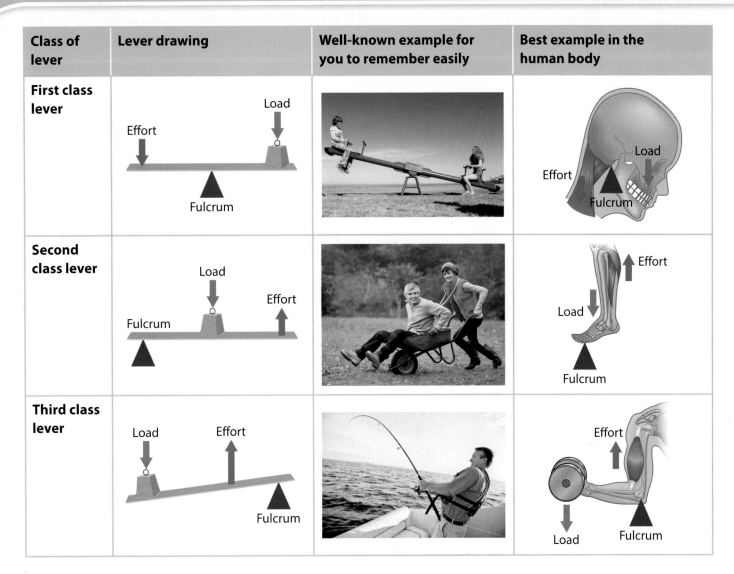 | | |
| **Second class lever** | | | |
| **Third class lever** | | | |

## Exam tip 🎯

It is important to think about where a muscle attaches to the bone when labelling the effort. This is especially key at the elbow. The biceps attach between the fulcrum (the elbow joint) and the load, meaning a biceps curl uses a third class lever. The triceps attach behind the fulcrum, meaning that a triceps extension uses a first class lever.

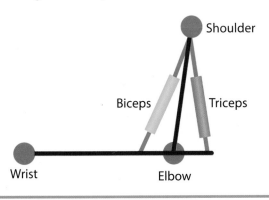

## Activities 🏃

2 Using a ruler, a rubber and a pencil, make a first class, second class and third class lever. You will need to act as the effort.

3 Experiment with the examples of levers in the human body given, to increase your understanding. Nod your head backwards and forwards imagining the pivot point in the middle (first class lever); move up and down on your tip toes pivoting on the ball of your foot (second class lever); and perform the upward phase of a biceps curl, recognising that your biceps muscle is pulling on your forearm (third class lever).

There are two main benefits of lever systems:

1   Large loads can be moved with a relatively small amount of effort.
2   The distance a load can be moved, or the speed with which it can be moved, can be increased without an increase in effort.

To work out the benefit of a particular lever, you need to look at the length of two arms. The distance from the load to the fulcrum is known as the **load arm**, while the distance from the effort to the fulcrum is known as the **effort arm**.

> ### Key terms
>
> **Load arm:** The distance from the load to the fulcrum.
>
> **Effort arm:** The distance from the effort to the fulcrum.

### Activity

4   Draw a simple diagram of each of the three lever classes and label the effort arm and load arm. Here is an example of a first class lever to show you how this is done.

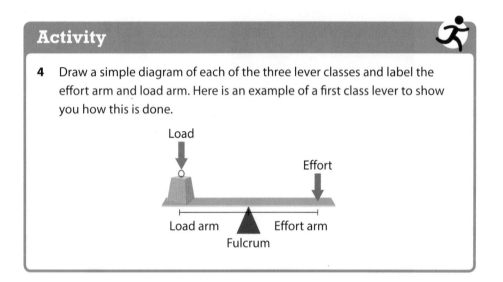

## Mechanical advantage and disadvantage

### Mechanical advantage

When a lever's effort arm is longer than its load arm it is said to have **mechanical advantage**. Levers with mechanical advantage can move large loads with a relatively small amount of effort. They have a high load force to effort ratio. Second class levers always have mechanical advantage.

If we consider a long jumper taking off, we see how the second class lever, where the foot contacts the ground, has a high mechanical advantage because the effort arm is longer than the load arm. The result of this, for the long jumper, is that the force produced by the muscles, which is relatively small, is able to drive the full weight of the athlete off the ground.

> ### Key term
>
> **Mechanical advantage:** Second class levers allow a large load to be moved with a relatively small amount of muscular effort.

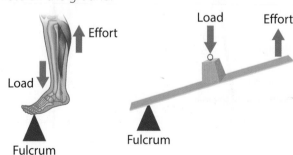

## Mechanical disadvantage

When a lever's load arm is longer than its effort arm, it is said to be at a **mechanical disadvantage.** It has a low load force to effort ratio. Third class levers always have mechanical disadvantage.

Despite operating at mechanical disadvantage, third class levers are able to increase the distance covered and, therefore, the speed at the end of a lever arm. They can produce a larger range of movement with relatively low effort.

The hip joint is a third class lever. It cannot produce the same load force to effort ratio as a second class lever. However, this doesn't mean that it is not good at what it does. Third class levers can take a small movement near the fulcrum and make a large movement where the load is. This provides a relatively large range of movement, which results in relatively high speed being produced.

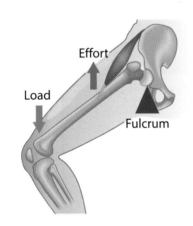
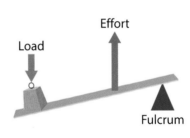

## First class levers: mechanical advantage and disadvantage

In the case of first class levers, the position of the fulcrum is key. If the fulcrum is closer to the load, then relatively low effort will result in larger, more powerful movements at the load end; there will be mechanical advantage. If the fulcrum is closer to the effort, then the lever will operate at mechanical disadvantage but will produce a larger range of movement at the end of the lever and greater speed as a result.

### Activity

5

a) Look at these rowers and discuss the class of lever that the oars create.
b) What is the benefit of this lever system to the rowers' performance?

**Planes** and **axes** can be used when describing movement patterns. A plane is an imaginary line or surface that divides the body into two. Movement occurs in a plane. An axis is an imaginary line around or about which the whole body or part of the body can turn.

Planes and axes are both drawn through a body standing in the anatomical position (upright, with arms by the side of the body and palms facing forwards). All movements are then described from this starting point.

### Key terms

**Plane:** An imaginary line dividing the body into two.

**Axis:** An imaginary line around which a body or body part can turn. "Axes" is the plural of axis.

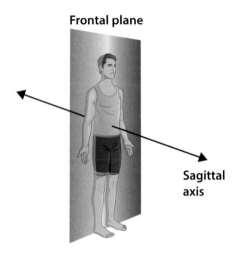

Frontal plane

Sagittal axis

◀ The **frontal plane** divides the body vertically from front to back. Movement occurs in the frontal plane about the sagittal axis. The **sagittal axis** passes horizontally through the body from front to back, allowing abduction and adduction.

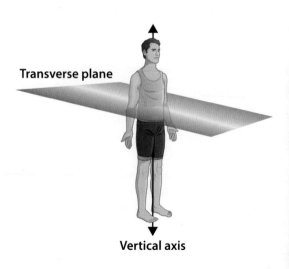

Transverse plane

Vertical axis

◀ The **transverse plane** divides the body horizontally from front to back. Movement occurs in the transverse plane about the vertical axis. The **vertical axis** passes vertically through the body, allowing rotation of the body in an upright position.

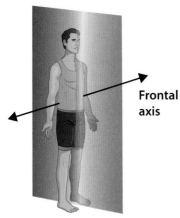

**Sagittal plane**

**Frontal axis**

▲ The **sagittal plane** divides the body vertically into left and right sides. Movement occurs in the sagittal plane about the frontal axis. The **frontal axis** passes horizontally through the body from left to right, allowing flexion and extension.

By looking at the diagrams and photographs together, we can see that:

- A cartwheel in gymnastics or dance takes place in the frontal plane around the sagittal axis.

- A full twist jump in trampolining takes place in the transverse plane around the vertical axis.

- A somersault in gymnastics or diving (front/back and piked/tucked) takes place in the sagittal plane around the frontal axis.

**Activity**

6 **a)** Make a model of a person standing in the anatomical position from Plasticine or Play-Doh. Use a pencil as an axis and two pieces of card as a plane. Push your pencil through your model and attach a piece of card to either side to represent the corresponding plane. If you spin your pencil, the model will rotate around that axis and in line with the plane.

**b)** Can you think of other sporting actions that take place in the planes and around the axes described on these two pages? They can be whole body movements or movements that involve only part of the body.

**c)** Use your model to make a video presentation explaining planes and axes, using the examples you came up with for part b.

**Exam tip**

A wheel on a bike spins around a central axle. This is how an axis works. If you had an axis through your belly button, you'd spin like a wheel.

Think of a plane as a thick sheet of glass that you're trapped tightly inside. Movements that take place in that plane can only occur in the direction that the sheet of glass allows.

# Exam-style questions

1 Which one of the following describes a third class lever? (1)
   A The load is to the right of the fulcrum
   B The effort is in the middle of the lever
   C The load is in the middle of the lever
   D The fulcrum is on the left of the lever

2 Which one of the following is an example of a first class lever? (1)
   A A car jack
   B A nutcracker
   C A wheelbarrow
   D A pair of tweezers

3 Which one of the following puts the correct plane and axis together? (1)
   A Sagittal plane with vertical axis
   B Sagittal plane with frontal axis
   C Transverse plane with sagittal axis
   D Frontal plane with frontal axis

4 Which one of the following levers provides mechanical advantage? (1)
   A First class lever where the fulcrum is exactly in the middle
   B First class lever where the fulcrum is nearer the effort
   C Third class lever
   D Second class lever

5 Identify the axis of movement for the cartwheel shown in **Figure 1**. (1)

▲ **Figure 1**

   A Vertical axis
   B Frontal axis
   C Sagittal axis
   D Transverse axis

6 **Figure 2** shows a high jumper during take off.

▲ **Figure 2**

Analyse how the following parts of the lever system, in the leg and where the foot contacts the ground, allow the high jumper to drive up and over the bar.
   a) Fulcrum (2)
   b) Effort (2)

7 When sprinting, the knee joint of a footballer uses a third class lever system.
   Examine the role of the lever in a footballer's running performance. (3)

8 Using examples, describe how mechanical advantage or disadvantage is determined in a lever system. (4)

9 Evaluate the extent to which second and third class levers impact the performance of a sprinter. (9)

10 Using examples, evaluate how knowledge of different movement planes and axes can assist a gymnast in performing specific movements correctly. (9)

# 3 Physical training

When you have worked through this chapter, you will have developed knowledge and understanding of:

- the relationship between health and fitness, and the role that exercise plays in both

- the components of fitness, their benefits for sport, and how fitness is measured and improved

- the principles of training and their application to personal exercise/training programmes

- the long-term effects of exercise

- how to optimise training and prevent injury

- effective use of warm up and cool down.

**Health** is a state of complete emotional, physical and social well-being, and not merely the absence of disease and infirmity. **Fitness** is the ability to meet the demands of the environment. You exercise in order to get fitter, which will help to maintain your health. As a result of being fit and healthy, you're in a position to maximise your performance. Being fit also contributes to both emotional and social well-being.

## Exam tip

Find out more about well-being and physical, emotional social health on pages 108–113.

**Exercise** is the name given to any form of physical activity done to maintain or improve your health or level of fitness. It is not competitive sport. The more you exercise, the fitter you become and the more able you are to **perform**, to take part in competitive sport and complete daily activities easily.

## Key terms

**Health:** A state of complete emotional, physical and social well-being, and not merely the absence of disease and infirmity.

**Fitness:** The ability to meet the demands of the environment.

**Exercise:** A form of physical activity done to maintain or improve health and/or fitness; it is not a competitive sport.

**Performance:** The action of performing a task, including a sporting performance.

## Exam tip

You need to be able to explain the relationship between health, fitness, exercise and performance. So learn these key terms, and think about how they relate to each other.

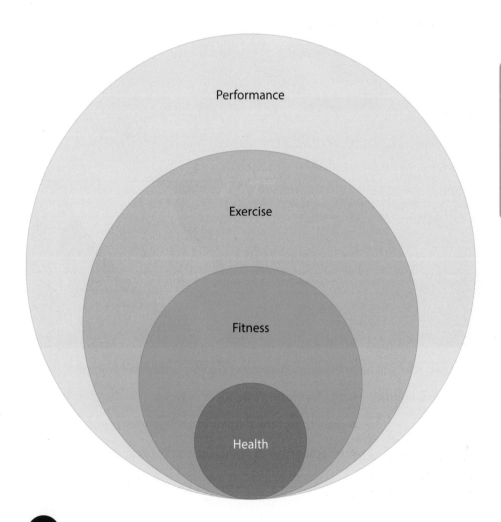

## The components of fitness

Fitness for sport can be broken down into 11 components:

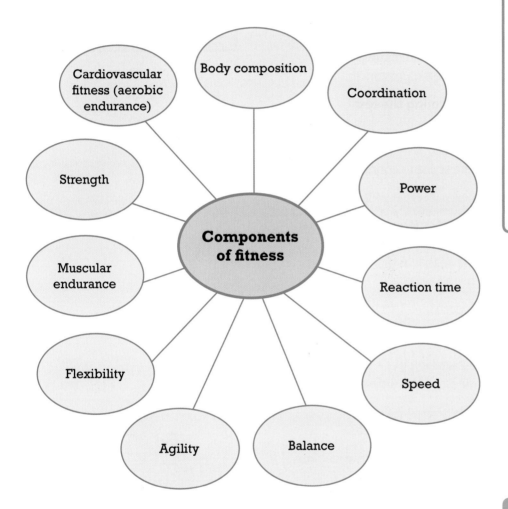

### Activity

1 Create a memory aid to help you remember the 11 components of fitness. A memory aid is a system that you use to help you remember something. For example, on page 7 we suggest you use the mnemonic "**B**ones **M**ake **M**oving **J**oints **Po**ssible" to help you recall the functions of the skeleton.

All performers need a good level of all 11 components of fitness, but different sports have different requirements. This means that one sport may need a much higher level of fitness in a specific component than another. So, for example, a gymnast will focus on developing flexibility in order to make movements look aesthetically pleasing and in order not to lose marks for poor execution, whereas a hammer thrower will focus on developing power to help increase the distance that they throw.

## Fitness testing

The purpose of fitness testing is to gather information about your current level of fitness in one or more of the 11 components of fitness. The results can then be used to put together a suitable Personal Exercise Programme (PEP). Re-testing every six to eight weeks will allow you to monitor your progress.

### Exam tip

Remember, a fitness test is *not* a training method. It is a test that measures fitness. Training methods are discussed on page 75.

### Exam tip

Guidance on how to develop a Personal Exercise Programme (PEP) is provided in Chapter 7.

Test protocols need to be put in place to ensure the appropriateness, safety and accuracy of each fitness test. Protocols are rules that must be followed.

## Four steps to successful fitness testing

### 1) Choose the right test

Identify the component of fitness that the participant wants to develop, and choose the fitness test that measures that particular component of fitness. If there is more than one fitness test that measures that component of fitness, consider the advantages and disadvantages of each, and choose the most appropriate for the circumstances.

### 2) Follow the standard method for performing the test

Follow the standard method for performing the test carefully to ensure that the results you collect are reliable and valid. Use the specified equipment, and ensure you have adequate space to conduct the test.

### 3) Make sure your tests are accurate

The results of fitness tests must be accurate in order to be useful. Often, the same participant will generate different results each time they take a test, and it is, therefore, important to ensure that as many factors as possible remain constant. Think about the following.

**a)** Have you used the same equipment each time? Is it working correctly?

**b)** Have you performed the test correctly each time?

**c)** Is the environment in which the test is taking place the same each time? For example, is the temperature, and the time of day the tests are performed, similar?

**d)** Is the participant's physical health the same each time?

**e)** Is the participant putting in the same amount of effort each time?

### 4) Be safe

Check the equipment carefully to ensure that it is safe to use, and ask the participant to sign a consent form.

## Activity

2   Using the information on pages 57–74 (the components of fitness and fitness tests that follow):
  **a)**  Identify the components of fitness that are essential to success in one of your favourite physical activities. Explain your decisions.
  **b)**  Choose fitness tests to assess the components of fitness that you identified in a). Explain your choices.
  **c)**  Perform the fitness tests you chose in b).
  **d)**  Evaluate the data you collect against **normative data**. Which of the components of fitness that you tested, do you need to improve?

## Key term

**Normative data:** Normative data shows the results for "normal" people. Data is collected from a large sample of people and the most common results are established.

**Cardiovascular fitness**, also known as aerobic endurance, is a measure of how efficiently your body can deliver oxygen and nutrients, such as glucose, to your working muscles during exercise. The ability to carry away waste products, such as carbon dioxide and lactic acid, is also part of cardiovascular fitness. This is crucial during physical activity, because the requirements for oxygen and nutrients go up when a person is exercising. The need to transport carbon dioxide and lactic acid away from the muscles also increases. The better your cardiovascular fitness, the longer you can keep going.

> **Exam tip**
>
> See pages 22–3 for more information on the cardiovascular system and its role in physical activity and sport.

◀ Cardiovascular fitness is especially important for endurance athletes such as Chris Froome.

## Testing cardiovascular fitness: Cooper 12-minute test

The Cooper 12-minute test measures how far you can run or swim in 12 minutes.

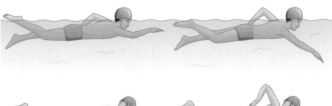

**What do you need?**

- 400 metre running track or 25 metre swimming pool
- Stopwatch
- Whistle
- Assistant

**How do you do the test?**

- Warm up for ten minutes.
- When your assistant gives the command "Go" and starts the stopwatch, run or swim laps for 12 minutes.

- Your assistant should provide you with the time remaining at the end of each lap or length.

- At the end of 12 minutes, your assistant should shout "Stop", and you should measure the distance covered during this time to the nearest 10 metres.

### Normative data for 15–16-year-olds

Running:

|  | Excellent | Above average | Average | Below average | Poor |
|---|---|---|---|---|---|
| **Male** | > 2800 m | 2500–2800 m | 2300–2499 m | 2200–2299 m | < 2200 m |
| **Female** | > 2100 m | 2000–2100 m | 1700–1999 m | 1600–1699 m | < 1600 m |

*Source: www.brianmac.co.uk*

Swimming:

|  | Excellent | Above average | Average | Below average | Poor |
|---|---|---|---|---|---|
| **Male** | > 725 m | 640–724 m | 550–639 m | 460–549 m | < 460 m |
| **Female** | > 640 m | 550–639 m | 460–549 m | 356–459 m | < 365 m |

*Source: Cooper, K. H., The Aerobics Program for Total Well-being, Bantam Books, 1982.*
*Data converted from yards to metres.*

**Exam tip** DATA 🎯

- > means "more than"
- < means "less than".

If the arrow starts off open, it means "more". If the arrow starts off closed, it means "less".

### Advantages of the Cooper 12-minute test

- Large groups can be tested at the same time.

- It is a simple test to perform.

### Disadvantages of the Cooper 12-minute test

- The accuracy of the test is dependent on the amount of practice a performer has done, their pacing strategies, and their level of motivation.

- You must have access to a 25 m swimming pool, or a 400 m running track.

- Keeping track of an individual's lap number can be difficult when there is a large group performing the test at the same time.

## Testing cardiovascular fitness: Harvard step test

### What do you need?

- A step (45 cm high)

- Metronome

- Stopwatch

- Assistant

### How do you do the test?

- Warm up for ten minutes.

- Set the metronome at 30 beats per minute.

- When your assistant gives the command "Go" and starts the stopwatch, step 30 steps per minute in time with the metronome.

- Continue stepping for five minutes, or until you are exhausted and cannot maintain the stepping rate for 15 seconds.

- Sit down when you have finished the test and measure the number of times your heart beats:

  - between 1.0 and 1.5 minutes after completing the test (Heart beats 1)

  - between 2.0 and 2.5 minutes after completing the test (Heart beats 2)

  - between 3.0 and 3.5 minutes after completing the test (Heart beats 3).

Record the results.

- Count your heart beats at your radial pulse by placing your index and middle finger on the inside of your wrist, or at your carotid pulse by placing your index and middle finger on either side of your neck. Do not press hard.

- Calculate your level of fitness using the following formula:

$$\frac{100 \times \text{duration of test in seconds}}{2 \times (\text{heart beats 1} + \text{heart beats 2} + \text{heart beats 3})}$$

**Normative data for 16-year-olds**

| | Excellent | Above average | Average | Below average | Poor |
|---|---|---|---|---|---|
| **Male** | > 90 | 80–89.9 | 65–79.9 | 55–64.9 | < 55 |
| **Female** | > 86 | 76–86 | 61–75.9 | 50–60.9 | < 50 |

*Source: Beashel, P. and Taylor, J., The World of Sport Examined, Thomas Nelson and Sons, 1997.*

### Advantages of the Harvard step test

- Minimal equipment and space is required.

- The test can be self-administered.

### Disadvantages of the Harvard step test

- The accuracy of the test is dependent on how strictly the instructions are followed and the performer's level of motivation.

- The height of the step will disadvantage a short person because they will need more energy to complete a step up than a taller person. Similarly, weight can affect performance because a heavier person will need more energy to complete a step than a lighter person.

- Testing large groups can be time consuming.

- There is a danger that the performer will trip if they are tired and cannot get their foot up onto the step.

**Strength** is the amount of force a muscle can generate when it contracts to overcome resistance. The stronger you are, the easier it is to do everyday tasks such as lifting and carrying.

## Testing strength: Grip dynamometer

### What do you need?

- A grip dynamometer

### How do you do the test?

- Use a grip dynamometer to measure grip strength.

- Record the maximum reading from three attempts using your dominant hand.

- Allow one-minute recovery time between each attempt.

- Grip strength is usually measured in kilograms (kg).

Key term

**Strength:** The amount of force a muscle can generate when it contracts to overcome resistance.

▲ Strength, especially in the fingers and forearms, is important for rock climbers if they are going to be able to pull hard on small or medium holds.

### Normative data for 16–19-year-olds

|  | Excellent | Above average | Average | Below average | Poor |
|---|---|---|---|---|---|
| **Male** | > 56 kg | 51–56 kg | 45–50 kg | 39–44 kg | < 39 kg |
| **Female** | > 36 kg | 31–36 kg | 25–30 kg | 19–24 kg | < 19 kg |

*Source: Davis, B. et al., Physical Education and the Study of Sport, 4th edition, Harcourt, 2000.*

### Advantages of the grip dynamometer

- It is a simple test, which is easy to conduct.

- There is a lot of normative data to use for comparison.

### Disadvantages of the grip dynamometer

- The dynamometer must be adjusted for hand size. How well this is done has an effect on the accuracy of the measurement.

- It only focuses on forearm and hand strength, and does not consider the strength of other parts of the body.

**Muscular endurance** is a measure of the length of time your voluntary muscles can contract without getting tired. This can be repeated muscle contractions, or one contraction held for a long period of time. The greater level of muscular endurance you have, the longer you can perform.

> ### Key term
>
> **Muscular endurance:** A measure of the length of time your voluntary muscles can contract without getting tired. This can be repeated muscle contractions, or one contraction held for a long period of time.

◀ Hockey players need muscular endurance to run around the pitch during a match and gymnasts need muscular endurance to maintain balance.

## Testing muscular endurance: One-minute sit-up test

### What do you need?

- Exercise mat
- Stopwatch
- Assistant

### How do you do the test?

- Lie on an exercise mat with your knees bent at right angles and your feet flat on the ground. Rest your hands on your thighs.

- Squeeze your stomach, push your lower back flat, and raise your upper body high enough for your hands to slide along your thighs to touch the tops of your knees. Don't pull with your neck or head, and keep your lower back on the floor. Then return to the starting position.

- Your assistant should count how many full sit-ups you can complete in one minute, or up to the point where you cannot continue.

### Normative data for 16–19-year-olds

|  | Excellent | Above average | Average | Below average | Poor |
|---|---|---|---|---|---|
| **Male** | > 30 | 26–30 | 20–25 | 17–19 | < 17 |
| **Female** | > 25 | 21–25 | 15–20 | 9–14 | < 9 |

*Source: Davis, B. et al., Physical Education and the Study of Sport, 4th edition, Harcourt, 2000.*

**Advantages of the one-minute sit-up test**

- It is simple to perform.

- It requires minimal equipment.

- Large groups can be tested at once.

**Disadvantage of the one-minute sit-up test**

- It is difficult to determine when a correct sit-up has been performed, and so there may be a dispute about the total number.

## Testing muscular endurance: One-minute press-up test

**What do you need?**

- Stopwatch

- Assistant

**How do you do the test?**

- Take up the starting position:
    - For a full press-up the starting position is with arms fully extended, body straight, hands slightly wider than shoulder-width apart, fingers pointing forwards, and both feet on the floor.
    - The starting position for a modified press-up (for those with less upper body strength) is with arms fully extended, body as straight as possible but with *knees on the ground*, weight over the hands, which are placed slightly wider than shoulder-width apart, and fingers pointing forwards.

- On the command "Go", bend your elbows and lower your body until your shoulders drop below the level of your elbows. Then return to the starting point. Pausing to rest is only allowed in the starting position.

- Your assistant should count how many full press-ups you can complete in one minute, or up to the point where you cannot continue.

▲ A normal press-up

▲ A modified press-up

**Normative data for 17–19-year-olds**

| | Excellent | Good | Above average | Average | Below average | Poor | Very poor |
|---|---|---|---|---|---|---|---|
| **Male (full press-up)** | > 56 | 47–56 | 35–46 | 19–34 | 11–18 | 4–10 | < 4 |
| **Female (modified press-up)** | > 35 | 27–35 | 21–27 | 11–20 | 6–10 | 2–5 | 0–1 |

Source: Golding, L.A. et al., The Y's Way to Physical Fitness, *3rd edition, 1986*

### Advantages of the one-minute press-up test

- The test is simple to perform.
- The test requires minimal equipment.

### Disadvantages of the one-minute press-up test

- It can be difficult to assess whether each press-up is performed correctly. This can lead to uncertainty about the total number completed.
- The performer will get tired if they stay in the ready position for too long. This can make it difficult to test a lot of people at the same time.

**Flexibility** is the ability of your joints to move through their full range of movement. The greater your flexibility, the more you are able to move your body effectively.

## Testing flexibility: Sit and reach test

### What do you need?

- A box and a measuring tape, or a sit and reach table

### How do you do the test?

- Sit comfortably on the floor with your legs straight out in front of you.

- Place the measuring tape, with 0 cm level with your feet, parallel with your legs. If you are using a sit and reach table, the measurements are already marked.

- Put the soles of your feet, shoulder width apart, against the box/table.

- Make sure your knees are straight, as this is what determines hamstring flexibility. If your knees bend during the test, the results will be inaccurate.

- With your hands stretched towards your feet, lean forwards and reach as far as possible with your fingertips. If possible, reach beyond the end of your toes and over the top of the box. You must make sure, however, that there are no jerky movements while doing this and that you are able to hold the reach for at least two seconds.

- You get three chances to stretch forwards and then the fourth stretch is measured.

- The distance that your fingers touch on the measuring tape/sit and reach table will be your score, showing the distance you were from 0 cm.

### Normative data for 16–19-year-olds

|  | Excellent | Above average | Average | Below average | Poor |
|---|---|---|---|---|---|
| **Male** | > 14 cm | 14–11 cm | 10.9–7 cm | 6.9–4 cm | < 4 cm |
| **Female** | > 15 cm | 15–12 cm | 11.9–7 cm | 6.9–4 cm | < 4 cm |

*Source: Davis, B. et al., Physical Education and the Study of Sport, 4th edition, Harcourt, 2000.*

**Key term**

**Flexibility:** The ability of your joints to move through their full range of movement.

▲ Dancers need flexibility in order to execute expressive movements.

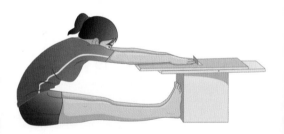

### Advantages of sit and reach test

- It is well known.

- It is easy and quick to perform.

- There is a lot of published data to use for comparison.

### Disadvantages of sit and reach test

- Variations in the length of individuals' arms, legs and trunk can make comparisons between people inaccurate.

- The test focuses only on the flexibility of the lower back and hamstrings.

**Body composition** is a measure of the percentages of fat, muscle, bone, water and vital organs that make up your body weight. You are born with a tendency towards a particular body composition, but exercise and diet can bring about changes. The important thing is that you have the correct body composition for your sport.

### Key term

**Body composition:** A measure of the percentages of fat, muscle, bone, water and vital organs that make up your body weight.

▼ High Jumpers, like Anna Chicherova, need to be tall and lean while 400 m runners, like Christine Ohuruogu, need to be muscular.

### Exam tip

You are not expected to know how to test body composition for the exam, but you may want to test it as part of your PEP. If you do, you could research how to use skinfold calipers or Bioelectrical Impedance Analysis (BIA) to test body composition.

**Agility** is a measure of how quickly you can change the position of your body, while keeping your entire body under control. Agility is influenced by a combination of speed and balance.

▼ Boxers, like Nicola Adams, need agility so that they can change body positions during a fight and avoid being punched by their opponent.

### Exam tip

You are not expected to know how to test agility for the exam, but you may want to test it as part of your PEP. If you do, you could research how to conduct the Illinois agility run test.

**Balance** is your ability to keep your body steady both when in a static position and when moving.

▼ Gymnasts perform balances that involve little or no movement. Netball players need good balance when they dodge around an opponent, changing position quickly.

### Key term

**Balance:** Your ability to keep your body steady both when in a static position and when moving.

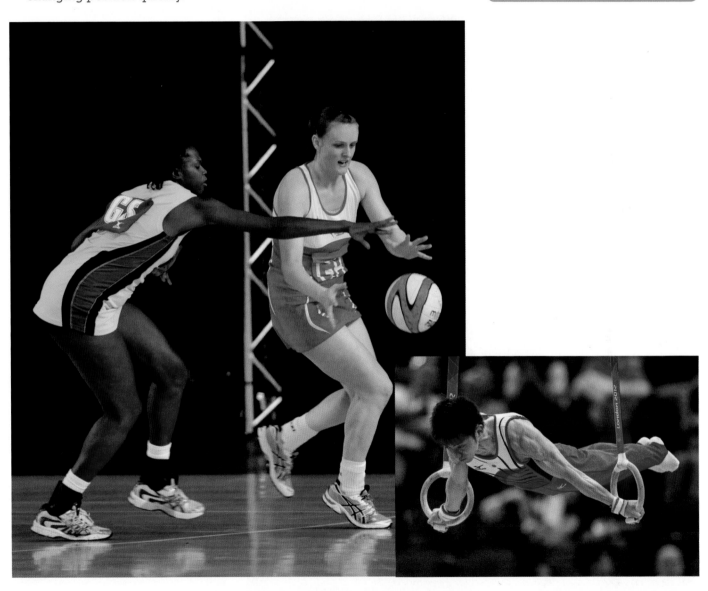

### Exam tip

You are not expected to know how to test balance for the exam, but you may want to test it as part of your PEP. If you do, you could research how to use the Stork balance test.

**Coordination** is your ability to move two or more body parts together, accurately and smoothly. The more coordinated you are, the easier you will find it to perform complex actions.

## Key term

**Coordination:** The ability to move two or more body parts together, accurately and smoothly.

▲ Tennis requires coordination of the hands, feet, legs and arms, head and trunk.

## Exam tip

You are not expected to know how to test coordination for the exam, but you may want to test it as part of your PEP. If you do, you could research how to use the Alternate hand wall toss test.

**Reaction time** is the amount of time it takes you to respond to a stimulus. A stimulus can be anything from a starting gun to a sudden side-step by an opponent or a shout from a teammate. The shorter your reaction time, the faster you will respond.

▼ The winner of a 100 m sprint can be determined in the very first seconds of the race. The person with the quickest reaction time responds fastest to the starting gun, and is out of the blocks before their competitors.

### Key term

**Reaction time:** The amount of time it takes you to respond to a stimulus.

### Exam tip

You are not expected to know how to test reaction time for the exam, but you may want to test it as part of your PEP. If you do, you could research how to use the Ruler drop test.

**Speed** is the rate at which your body, or part of your body, is able to perform a movement.

$$\text{Speed} = \frac{\text{Distance}}{\text{Time}}$$

▲ In a sprint canoe race, the canoeist needs to transfer their upper body forwards as fast as possible. A canoeist digs the paddle into the water, and then pulls the paddle towards the body quickly in order to cover maximum distance in one stroke.

## Testing speed: 30 m sprint test

The 30 m sprint test measures your acceleration and maximum speed.

### What do you need?

- Measuring tape

- Stopwatch

- Cone markers

- Flat and clear surface of at least 50 m, marked with a start line and a finish line 30 m away

- Assistant

## How do you do the test?

- Warm up for ten minutes.

- Start from a stationary position, with one foot in front of the other and with the front foot on or behind the starting line. Hold the position for at least two seconds before starting, and do not rock backwards and forwards.

- Run, as fast as you can, to the finish line. Your assistant should time you. The timing starts from your first movement and finishes when your chest crosses the finish line.

- You have two attempts and the best time is recorded in seconds, to one decimal place.

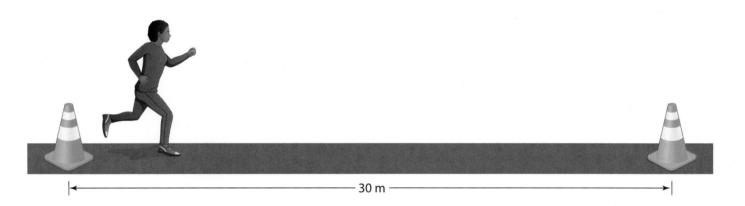

## Normative data for 16–19-year-olds

|  | Excellent | Above average | Average | Below average | Poor |
|---|---|---|---|---|---|
| **Male** | < 4 sec | 4.2–4 sec | 4.4–4.3 sec | 4.6–4.5 sec | > 4.6 sec |
| **Female** | < 4.5 sec | 4.6–4.5 sec | 4.8–4.7 sec | 5–4.9 sec | > 5 sec |

*Source: Davis, B. et al., Physical Education and the Study of Sport, 4th edition, Harcourt, 2000.*

## Advantages of the 30 m sprint test

- The test is quick to conduct.

- It can be performed anywhere that there is a flat surface that is 50 m long.

## Disadvantages of the 30 m sprint test

- The running surface and weather conditions (if conducted outside) can affect the results.

- The results can be inaccurate if a stopwatch is used, because there will be a slight delay as the assistant registers the beginning and end of the test. The test can be made more accurate if a timing gate is used.

**Power** is the ability to combine strength with speed to perform a strong muscular contraction very quickly.

## Testing power: Vertical jump test

### What do you need?

- Wall

- Measuring tape

- Chalk

- Assistant

### How to do the test?

- Stand side-on to a wall and reach up with the hand closest to the wall. Keeping your feet flat on the ground, your assistant should mark or measure the point on the wall where the top of the fingertip of your longest finger touches. This is your standing reach.

- Put a little chalk on your fingertips. Stand away from the wall and jump vertically as high as possible using both your arms and your legs to help you project your body upwards. Touch the wall at the highest point of the jump and have this marked or recorded.

- The difference in distance between the standing reach height and the jump height is your score.

> **Key term**
>
> **Power:** The ability to combine strength with speed to perform a strong muscular contraction very quickly.

▲ Rory McIlroy needs power to perform an effective golf swing.

### Normative data for 16–19-year-olds

|  | Excellent | Above average | Average | Below average | Poor |
|---|---|---|---|---|---|
| **Male** | > 65 cm | 50–65 cm | 40–49 cm | 30–39 cm | < 30 cm |
| **Female** | > 58 cm | 47–58 cm | 36–46 cm | 26–35 cm | < 26 cm |

*Source: Davis, B. et al., Physical Education and the Study of Sport, 4th edition, Harcourt, 2000.*

### Advantages of the vertical jump test

- It is quick and easy to perform.

### Disadvantages of the vertical jump test

- Technique plays a big part in achieving a good score, because the performer must mark the wall at the top of the jump.

Regardless of their level of performance, everybody who commits time to training wants to see improvements. In order to make progress during a Personal Exercise Programme (PEP), you must apply the **principles of training**.

Effective training results in adaptations to your body. Adaptations are positive changes that result in improved performance. A programme that does not apply the principles of training will be less effective and may not result in improvements in performance. Successful athletes do not just train hard, they also train effectively; they apply the principles of training.

## Key term

**Principles of training:** Guidelines that, if applied, ensure that training is effective and results in positive adaptations. The principles of training are: individual needs, specificity, progressive overload (FITT), overtraining and reversibility.

▲ Sprinters who carry out effective training will have increased quadriceps strength and will generate more speed, making them more competitive.

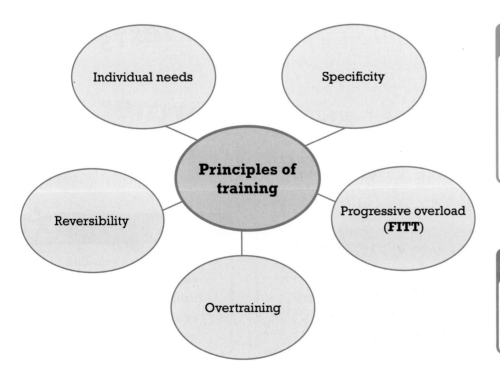

## Key term

**FITT:** This stands for **F**requency, **I**ntensity, **T**ime and **T**ype. The FITT principle should be used to ensure that a Personal Exercise Programme (PEP) delivers progressive overload.

## Activity

3   Create a mnemonic to help you remember the principles of training.

No two Personal Exercise Programmes should be exactly the same, because a PEP should be designed to meet the needs of the individual to ensure they are appropriately challenged. Factors to consider include:

Current level of fitness and history of physical activity

General health and well-being, including any medical problems that will impact on the performer's ability to exercise

Long-term goals

**Age**

The performer's attitude towards exercise, including their likes and dislikes and level of motivation

The amount of time and money the performer has to spend on exercise

The sports the participant takes part in or would like to take part in

The results of fitness tests

Gender

The performer's access to facilities

## Exam tip

Asking a performer to complete a **P**hysical **A**ctivity **R**eadiness **Q**uestionnaire (PARQ), which assesses an individual's readiness for training, can provide valuable information to help you design a PEP that meets an individual's needs. There is more about PARQ forms on page 93.

## Activity

4   What are your individual needs? Work with a partner, interview each other and establish your individual needs.

In order for a training programme to be effective, it must be specific. **Specificity** means that training should be matched to the requirements of the activity the performer is involved in.

Training should focus on the requirements of the activity. For example, someone who has started fitness training in order to lose weight should focus on exercises that improve their cardiovascular fitness and muscular endurance. A gymnast will need to incorporate flexibility training into their programme to ensure that they have a good range of movement when performing their routines. In team sports, different positions may require different training programmes: in rugby union, a prop forward requires a high level of muscular strength and power, while a winger has a greater need for speed and agility.

Training should also take place in an appropriate setting. You might think it is obvious that swimmers do most of their training in the pool, cyclists do most of their training on a bike, and footballers do most of their training on a football pitch, but these are all examples of performers applying the principle of specificity.

## Key term

**Specificity:** Training should be matched to the requirements of the activity that the performer is involved in.

## Exam tip

Designing an exercise programme for a performer? Be specific!

- Train the appropriate muscle groups (see page 86).

- Train the appropriate components of fitness (see pages 59–74).

- Train in the appropriate target training zone (see pages 78–80).

## Activity

5 What components of fitness do Usain Bolt and Mo Farrah need in order to compete successfully? How is this important when designing their training programmes?

**Progressive overload** is about training harder as time passes. The demands placed on your body should gradually increase during a PEP to ensure that you continue to adapt. If your body is not progressively overloaded, no further improvements will take place and your levels of fitness will plateau.

The **FITT** principle should be used to ensure that a PEP incorporates progressive overload.

> ## Key term
>
> Progressive overload: The frequency, intensity, time and/or type of exercise are gradually increased to ensure that levels of fitness continue to improve.

| **F**requency | How often training takes place each week | For example:<br>• Increase training sessions from two to three times per week |
| --- | --- | --- |
| **I**ntensity | How hard the exercise is | For example:<br>• Increase resistance (e.g. increasing weight lifted)<br>• Increase the effort put in (e.g. increasing the incline on a running machine) |
| **T**ime | The length of the session or of a particular exercise | For example:<br>• Increase sets<br>• Increase repetitions<br>• Decrease rest time<br>• Increase overall length of training session |
| **T**ype | The method of training used | For example:<br>• Switch between continuous training, interval training and Fartlek training or between running and swimming to improve cardiovascular fitness (see pages 83–4). |

## Thresholds of training

One of the most effective ways to measure intensity – and to ensure you are working hard enough to make fitness gains – is to calculate your minimum and maximum thresholds of training, and ensure that you work within your target training zone.

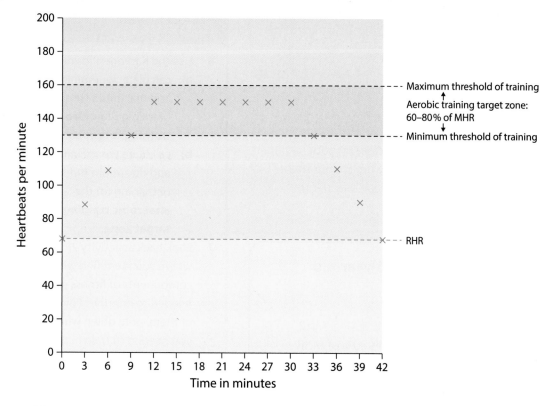

◀ A graph to illustrate the changes in heart rate when a 20-year-old male performs continuous training in the aerobic training target zone.

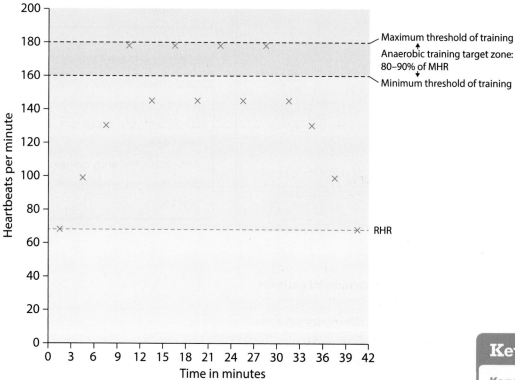

◀ A graph to illustrate the changes in heart rate when a 20-year-old male performs interval training. The work takes place in the anaerobic training zone and the active recovery takes place in the aerobic training zone.

The **Karvonen formula** can be used to calculate your aerobic and anaerobic target training zones:

Target Heart Rate = ((MHR − RHR) × %Intensity) + RHR

### Key term

**Karvonen formula:** Target Heart Rate = ((MHR − RHR) × %Intensity) + RHR.

(MHR = Maximum Heart Rate, calculated as 220 − age. RHR = Resting Heart Rate.)

Maximum Heart Rate (MHR) is calculated as follows:

MHR = 220 − age

Resting Heart Rate (RHR) is calculated as follows:

In a state of rest, find your pulse at either the carotid artery (in your neck) or the radial artery (in your wrist) and count how many times your heart beats in one minute. This is your resting heart rate in beats per minute (bpm).

---

### Calculating the aerobic training zone for a 16-year-old

MHR = 220 − 16 = 204
RHR = 68 bpm
The minimum threshold for the aerobic training zone is 60% of MHR.
The maximum threshold for the aerobic training zone is 80% of MHR.

Therefore, the target heart rate for the minimum threshold of the aerobic training zone = ((204 − 68) × 60%) + 68
= (136 × 0.6) + 68
= 81.6 + 68
= 149.6 bpm, rounded to 150 bpm

Therefore, the target heart rate for the maximum threshold of the aerobic training zone = ((204 − 68) × 80%) + 68
= (136 × 0.8) + 68
= 108.8 + 68
= 176.8 bpm, rounded to 177 bpm

This means that a 16-year-old with a resting heart rate of 68 bpm should work at between 150 and 177 beats per minute to train in the aerobic training target zone.

---

### Activities

6   Use the Karvonen formula to:
   a)   calculate your minimum and maximum thresholds of training for the **aerobic training target zone**.
   b)   calculate your minimum and maximum thresholds of training for the **anaerobic training target zone**.

7   Look back at activity 2, where you identified which components of fitness you needed to improve. For each of them, note down whether you needed to train in the aerobic target training zone or the anaerobic target training zone in order to improve.

### Key terms

**Aerobic training target zone:** 60–80% of your maximum heart rate.

**Anaerobic training target zone:** 80–90% of your maximum heart rate.

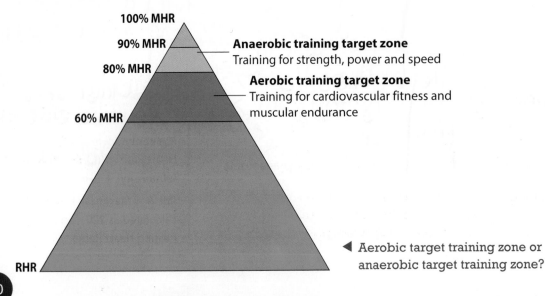

◀ Aerobic target training zone or anaerobic target training zone?

# 3.18 Overtraining

**Overtraining** occurs when you train too hard and do not give your body enough rest and recovery time between training sessions. Symptoms of overtraining include:

- constant thirst

- muscle soreness over 72 hours after a training session

- frequent illness

- an increase in the number of injuries

- lack of progress.

So how much is too much? Your level of fitness and the type of training you are doing influences how much is too much. Applying the principle of progressive overload and giving your body time to rest and recover between training sessions will help you to avoid overtraining.

▲ If you are training for a marathon, you need to increase the frequency of your training sessions gradually and also the distance, length of time and speed at which you run in order to make continuous gains in muscular endurance.

# 3.19 Reversibility

If you are unable to exercise, because of illness or injury or other commitments, any adaptions made as a result of training will be reversed. This is the principle of **reversibility**. Training regularly will help you to avoid reversibility.

However, it is important to understand that returning to training too quickly after illness or injury – and training at the same level as you were before you were sick or injured – will lead to overtraining and, in turn, to more illness or injury. You must return to training gradually, building up to your previous level of training as your fitness returns.

## Activity

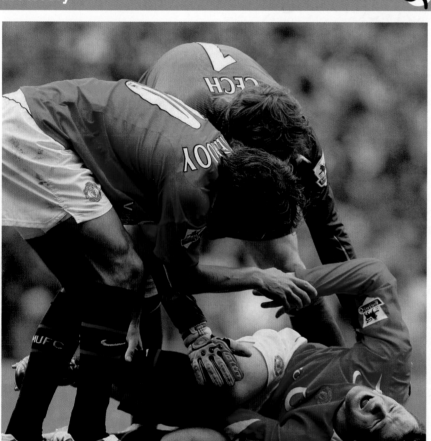

**8** When Wayne Rooney fractured the base of his fourth metatarsal in April 2006, it looked as if he wouldn't play in the 2006 FIFA World Cup. However, it took him just six weeks to recover thanks to a progressive training programme, and he was fit to play in England's second match against Trinidad and Tobago.

Why was it important to consider the principle of reversibility when designing Wayne Rooney's training programme?

The three types of cardiovascular fitness training that you need to know are: continuous training, Fartlek training and interval training.

◄ Olympic triathletes, the Brownlee brothers, need excellent cardiovascular fitness to be able to compete in a 1.5 km swim, a 40 km bike ride, and a 10 km run in less than two hours.

## Continuous training

Continuous training is taking part in a physical activity, such as jogging, running, swimming, cycling or rowing, for an extended period of time without rest.

Beginners should start with 20 minutes of continuous training, working in the aerobic training target zone, building up to training continuously for 30–45 minutes two to three times per week.

**Advantages of continuous training**

- Doesn't require expensive equipment.

- Ideal for beginners because it is easy to do.

- Ideal for elite performers during pre-season training to prepare their bodies for what lies ahead.

- Can mimic some aspects of a long-distance run.

**Disadvantages of continuous training**

- Can get boring.

- Does not improve anaerobic fitness.

## Interval training

Interval training consists of periods of work followed by periods of active recovery. During periods of work, you should work at between 80–90% of your Maximum Heart Rate, in the anaerobic training target zone, and during periods of rest or active recovery your heart rate should drop down into the aerobic training target zone. In other words, you alternate between training above and below the minimum threshold of your anaerobic training target zone. The length of the work intervals is determined by the performer's fitness level.

Working regularly anaerobically for short periods of time, around the minimum threshold of your anaerobic training target zone, increases the maximum threshold of the aerobic training target zone. It increases your ability to cope with the production of lactic acid and, therefore, increases your ability to work aerobically for longer.

When designing an interval training programme, consider the following:

- the intensity/speed of the work interval
- the distance or time of the work interval
- the distance or time of the rest/active recovery interval
- the number of repetitions of the intervals.

It is essential that the work interval mimics the physical demands that the performer will experience in their sport. For example, interval training for a football player should contain short work intervals at high intensity because footballers do not have to sprint over large distances continuously, but when they do they have to be able to run quickly.

The nature of the recovery interval and the number of repetitions depends on the performer's fitness. The fitter the performer, the shorter and more active the recovery intervals, and the more repetitions they should complete.

### Advantages of interval training

- You burn about twice as many calories interval training than you do continuous training.
- It is easy to see how hard the performer is working.
- It is easy to measure progress and improvement.

### Disadvantages of interval training

- Because it is a high intensity workout, your recovery period between interval training sessions should be at least 48 hours. Otherwise you are at risk of overtraining (see page 81).
- Because it is a high intensity workout, it can be difficult to keep going so you need self-motivation and self-discipline.

## Fartlek training

Fartlek is a Swedish term meaning "speed play". It is a form of interval training.

The performer alters the intensity of the exercise – their speed – over varying distances. A training session might consist of a jog for 60 seconds, followed by a hard run for 30 seconds, followed by a jog for 30 seconds, followed by an all-out sprint for 10 seconds, followed by a walk for 30 seconds, for as long as the performer wants. There are no rest sessions, just active recovery sessions where the exercise is performed at a lower intensity. Landmarks, such as street lights or trees, can be used to trigger a change of speed.

Remember there are no rest periods in Fartlek training sessions, just low intensity exercise such as walking or slow pedalling to help recover from speed work.

### Advantages of Fartlek training

- It is less boring than continuous and interval training.
- It can be completed anywhere.
- The performer develops pace-setting skills, which can be critical in long-distance events.
- The intensity of the exercise and the length of the training session can be modified by the performer, depending on their needs.

### Disadvantages of Fartlek training

- The performer has to be experienced to ensure the workout is intense but not too intense.
- The performer has to be self-motivated to push themselves to change pace regularly.
- It is difficult to observe the performer to establish how hard they are working and to measure progress over time.

> **Activity**
>
> 9   Take part in a continuous training session, an interval training session and a Fartlek training session. Can you add any more advantages and disadvantages to the lists?

When training for power it is more important to focus on the quality of the exercise than on the quantity. It is also vital that a performer has established strength and speed before considering power training, to avoid injury.

 Jessica Ennis-Hill includes a lot of different plyometric drills in her training programme in order to improve her leg and upper body power. She needs lots of explosive power in all seven events in the heptathlon, especially in the jumping and throwing events.

## Activity

10 Take part in a plyometrics training session. Make sure you warm up properly and focus on the quality of each exercise. Can you add any more advantages and disadvantages to the lists?

## Plyometrics

Plyometric exercises are high-impact exercises that teach the muscles to perform their maximum contractions faster; to be more powerful. They are used by performers who want to jump higher, run faster or throw further, and include:

▲ Clap press-ups

▲ Squat jumps

▲ Barrier jumps

Beginners should start with one session a week consisting of 40 repetitions, divided into sets. An advanced athlete can perform 120 to 200 repetitions, again divided into sets, three to four times a week. Rest of at least a minute between sets is required.

### Advantages of plyometrics

- Many plyometric exercises require little or no equipment.

- A plyometric workout is a short, high intensity work out.

- Plyometric exercises simulate the types of movements you make in your sport.

### Disadvantages of plyometrics

- You must have three days of recovery between each plyometrics training session.

- The performer must have good levels of strength and muscular endurance before attempting plyometrics.

- Repetitive bounding can cause stress on the joints and muscle soreness after training.

When training for strength, a performer will need to perform a lower number of repetitions using heavier weights.

When training for muscular endurance, a performer will need to perform a higher number of repetitions using lighter weights.

### Weight/resistance training

Free weights include dumbbells, barbells and kettlebells. Experienced performers tend to prefer using free weights because they are not limited to specific movements and their core muscles also have to work hard to keep them stable. However, exercises using free weights must be performed correctly to ensure the right muscles are being trained and to prevent injuries.

In contrast, resistance machines are ideal for performers new to the gym because they promote good technique by providing stability and controlling movements.

▲ Cyclists, like Chris Hoy, include weight training in their training programme to build both strength and muscular endurance in their legs so they can continuously pedal at a fast rate.

If completing a full body workout, it is best to work the larger muscles in the legs, back and chest first because you have the most amount of energy at the beginning of your workout, which limits your risk of injury. Then train the smaller muscles, such as the biceps and triceps and the muscles in your shoulders. It is a good idea to alternate muscle groups and rest between sets, so your muscles have time to recover.

It is also important to allow your muscles time to recover after training. A minimum of 48 hours is needed between weight/resistance training sessions, and the harder you work your muscles the longer they need to recover.

**Advantages of weight/resistance training:**

- Can be tailored to individual needs so it is appropriate for all levels.

- Can include a variety of exercises and different equipment to maintain interest and prevent boredom.

- Can strengthen the whole body but training can also be targeted at specific muscles.

- Most gyms insist on an induction session so you are taught how to use the resistance machines safely.

**Disadvantages of weight/resistance training:**

- Requires a lot of equipment and it can be expensive to join a gym.

- Incorrect technique, especially when using free weights, can lead to injury.

- You must have a spotter working with you if you want to lift heavy free weights.

### Activity

**11** Take part in a whole body weight/resistance training session. Remember it is important to use the correct technique and to warm up and cool down properly. Can you add any more advantages and disadvantages to the lists?

Circuit training can improve muscular strength, muscular endurance or cardiovascular fitness, depending on the exercises included in the circuit.

Circuit training involves six to ten different exercises, called stations, which are completed one after another. You perform each exercise for a set number of repetitions or for a set period of time before moving on to the next exercise after a brief, timed rest. When you have finished all the exercises, you have completed one circuit and there is usually a slightly longer rest period.

The number of stations, the time exercising and the time resting, as well as the number of circuits can be modified according to your level of fitness and the component(s) of fitness you want to train.

When planning a circuit, it is important not to have two consecutive exercises that train the same muscle group because you need to avoid muscle fatigue. For example, a plank hold could be followed by lunges rather than push ups.

Circuit training can be carried out two to three times per week with at least 48 hours rest between each session. Remember, the harder the muscles are worked, the more recovery time is required.

## Advantages of circuit training

- It is creative and fun.
- You can match the exercises to your specific training needs.
- Large groups can train at the same time.
- It does not require a lot of equipment or space; it can be done anywhere.
- It doesn't take long to complete one circuit.
- Performers with different fitness levels can train together.

## Disadvantages of circuit training

- It can take a while to set up, if it involves a lot of equipment.
- Technique can be affected by fatigue if performing as many reps as possible in a set amount of time, which can increase the risk of injury.

**Activity**

12 Plan, set up and complete a ten-station circuit. Remember that each station should exercise a different muscle group. Can you add any more advantages and disadvantages to the lists?

Fitness classes are a great way to improve a range of components of fitness and popular classes include:

### BodyPump

BodyPump is a weights-based group exercise class. It improves the strength of all the major muscles in the body.

### Aerobics

Aerobics involves participants completing rhythmical dance movements set to music. It combines a mixture of high and low intensity moves to improve cardiovascular fitness.

### Pilates

Pilates is an exercise system that develops strength and flexibility in the whole body. It focuses on the core muscles and on improving posture.

## Yoga

Yoga involves performing a series of postures that develop strength and flexibility in the whole body while paying attention to your breathing.

## Spinning

Spinning is a high intensity workout on stationary bikes. It improves cardiovascular fitness.

## Advantages of fitness classes

- There is lots of variety, reducing the likelihood of boredom.
- A good instructor will challenge you and motivate you to work harder.
- It's a great way to meet new people.
- It's a great way to exercise, if you do not have the knowledge to develop your own training programme.

## Disadvantages of fitness classes

- Attending fitness classes regularly can be expensive.
- Group classes are not tailored to the individual needs of performers and can neglect the very fit or the very unfit.
- In large classes, the instructor may not always be able to correct poor technique.

### Activity

13 Take part in an exercise class that you have never taken part in before. What do you like about it? What don't you like so much about it? Would you consider making it a regular part of your PEP?

### Activity DATA

14 Analyse the data you collected for activity 2 and:
   a) Choose one or more methods of training to improve the components of fitness you have identified that you need to improve.
   b) Decide how you will apply the principles of specificity and progressive overload to your chosen methods of training to create a six- to eight-week PEP. Remember not to overtrain.

Regular aerobic and anaerobic exercise has significant positive long-term effects on your **musculo-skeletal system** and your **cardio-respiratory system**. The adaptations that take place as a result of regular exercise ensure you can work for longer and at a higher intensity. An adaptation is a positive physical change that will help in developing your performance.

### Exam tip

Remember the principle of reversibility (see page 82). Adaptations are not permanent. They will reverse if you do not continue training.

## The long-term effects of exercise on the musculo-skeletal system

There are three adaptations to the musculo-skeletal system that take place as a result of regular exercise:

| Adaptation | Examples of benefits for performance |
| --- | --- |
| **1. Increased bone density**<br><br>The bones are put under stress during exercise and they adapt by becoming thicker and heavier (more dense) to prevent fractures occurring. | Gymnasts need strong bones because they tend to fall a lot when learning new skills. If they had weak bones, they would suffer from a lot of fractures. |
| **2. Increased strength of ligaments and tendons**<br><br>Ligaments and tendons are stretched during exercise and they adapt by becoming thicker and stronger to prevent them from tearing. | A basketball player needs strong tendons and ligaments because they need to change direction quickly and jump, which puts a lot of pressure on the tendons and ligaments in the knees and ankles. |
| **3. Muscle hypertrophy**<br><br>When a muscle is trained, small tears are created. As they heal, they develop and become thicker. This process is called hypertrophy, and it means that muscles adapt to exercise by increasing in size and producing greater strength. | A rower needs large muscles that produce high levels of strength in their upper and lower body to be able to overcome the resistance provided by the water. |

Adaptations to the musculo-skeletal system take place during periods of rest. This is why it is important to ensure you do not overtrain (see page 81), and that you give your body time to rest and recover between training sessions. This is also why overtraining can lead to a lack of progress; your body simply does not have the time to adapt.

### Key terms

**Musculo-skeletal system:** The name given to the combined body system that involves your muscles and your skeleton.

**Cardio-respiratory system:** The name given to the combined body system that involves your cardiovascular system and your respiratory system.

# The long-term effects of exercise on the cardio-respiratory system

There are five adaptations to the cardio-respiratory system that take place as a result of regular aerobic and anaerobic exercise:

| Adaptation | Benefits for performance |
|---|---|
| **1. Cardiac hypertrophy**<br><br>When you exercise regularly your heart, just like your voluntary muscles, increases in size and becomes stronger. | Cardiac hypertrophy has an impact on the values in the cardiac equation:<br><br>The cardiac equation:<br><br>stroke volume (SV) $\times$ heart rate (HR) = cardiac output (Q)<br><br>When your heart is stronger, it is able to pump out more blood per beat, even when you are resting. This means it does not have to work as hard and your Resting Heart Rate lowers.<br><br>Because your resting stroke volume increases, your maximum cardiac output also increases. Your heart is able to deliver more blood, and therefore more oxygen, to your working muscles and remove more carbon dioxide and other waste products, such as lactic acid. |
| **2. Increase in the elasticity of the muscular walls of the arteries and veins** | The more elastic the muscular walls of the veins and arteries, the more they can dilate and constrict. Oxygen is delivered to the working muscles faster and your resting blood pressure drops. |
| **3. Increase in the number of red blood cells** | Red blood cells carry oxygen to working muscles. The more red blood cells a performer has, the more oxygen can be carried to their working muscles. |
| **4. Capilliarisation and an increase in the number of alveoli** | Capilliarisation results in an increase in the number of capillaries wrapping around the alveoli. The number of alveoli also increases in the lungs. More capillaries and alveoli mean that a greater level of gaseous exchange can take place. A performer is, therefore, able to deliver more oxygen to their working muscles and remove waste products more quickly. Consequently, they can work aerobically for longer. |
| **5. Increased strength of the diaphragm and intercostal muscles leads to an increase in tidal volume and vital capacity** | An increase in the strength of the diaphragm and intercostal muscles has an impact on the respiratory equation:<br><br>The respiratory equation:<br><br>tidal volume (TV) $\times$ frequency (f) = minute ventilation (VE)<br><br>When your diaphragm and intercostal muscles are stronger, you can breathe more deeply. This increases your tidal volume; the amount of air you can inhale and exhale with each breath. It also increases your vital capacity; the maximum amount of air exhaled following a maximum inhalation. As a consequence, more oxygen can be brought into the body and delivered to working muscles. |

▲ Together, the long-term effects of exercise on the cardio-respiratory system improve a performer's aerobic capacity. This means they can perform longer before fatigue sets in, and their recovery time is shorter.

### Exam tip

There is a link between the short-term effects of exercise and the long-term effects of exercise. Look back at the short-term effects of exercise on the cardiac system (pages 38–9), respiratory system (pages 40–1) and vascular system (pages 42–3).

### Activity

**15** Design a slide presentation to explain the relationship between the short-term and long-term effects of exercise on the musculo-skeletal system and the cardio-respiratory system. Make sure to include images and, if possible, video clips in your presentation.

# 3.26 PARQ

**PARQ** stands for **P**hysical **A**ctivity **R**eadiness **Q**uestionnaire. Before taking part in fitness tests or physical exercise, all performers must complete a PARQ. This examines a performer's readiness for training and will flag up health conditions and lifestyle choices that may impact on the success of a Personal Exercise Programme (PEP). The PEP can then be designed with the individual needs of the performer in mind. For example, a PEP for a performer who suffers from severe back pain should not contain high-impact exercises.

Here is an example of a PARQ:

**Activity**

16 Have a look at some different PARQs and then design your own. Ask one male and one female to fill in your PARQ. Analyse each questionnaire and identify the areas that you would need to consider before designing a PEP.

## Physical Activity Readiness Questionnaire

Please take a few minutes to answer the following questions.

Name: _____ DOB: ___/___/___
Age: _____ Sex: M/F

Occupation: _____
Have you used a gym before? Y/N

Emergency contact: _____
Relationship: _____ Telephone number: _____

### Part A: Medical considerations

It is our professional duty to ask all participants, no matter what age, to complete the following questions. Please tick all those that apply.

Do you have or have you ever had:

☐ Gout ☐ Glandular fever ☐ Heart condition ☐ Stroke

☐ Rheumatic fever ☐ Heart murmur ☐ Diabetes

☐ Dizziness or fainting ☐ High blood pressure (over 140/90)

☐ Epilepsy ☐ Stomach/duodenal ulcer

☐ Palpitations or pains in the chest ☐ Hernia

☐ Liver or kidney condition ☐ Raised cholesterol/triglycerides

☐ Asthma ☐ Arthritis ☐ Muscular pain ☐ Cramps

Do you have any pain or major injuries in the following areas:

☐ Neck ☐ Knees ☐ Back ☐ Ankles

Please give details of any conditions:

_____

If you have ticked any of the above, you need a signed medical clearance from your doctor before starting exercise.

Doctor's signature: _____
Date: ___/___/___

I warrant that I am physically and mentally well enough to proceed with usage of the facility.

Client's signature: _____
Date: ___/___/___

### Part B: Lifestyle and current exercise habits

Are you currently exercising regularly? Yes ☐ No ☐

If yes, please give details below:

* Type of exercise: _____

* Frequency of exercise (times per week):

1 ☐ 2–3 ☐ 3–4 ☐ 5+ ☐

Do you currently drink more than the average amount of alcohol per week (21 units for men and 14 units for women (1 unit = pint of beer/cider/lager or 1 small glass of wine))? Yes ☐ No ☐

Do you currently smoke? Yes ☐ No ☐

Are you, or is there any possibility that you might be, pregnant? Yes ☐ No ☐

Do you know of any other reason why you should not participate in a programme of physical activity? Yes ☐ No ☐

Getting injured from playing sport or taking part in physical activity is not inevitable. Following these six simple rules will help optimise training and avoid injury.

**Rule 2**

**Make sure you understand and follow all the rules of an activity during play/participation.**

**Rule 1**

**Make sure your training programme is designed using the principles of training to avoid overuse injuries. Overuse injuries include tennis elbow and golfer's elbow.**

**Rule 3**

**Make sure you use appropriate protective clothing and equipment during play/participation.**

### Rule 4

**Always check equipment before use to make sure it is in good condition.**

### Activity

**17** Write a short report evaluating how the rules of one of your chosen physical activities protect participants from injury.

### Rule 5

**Always check facilities before use to make sure there are no hazards, such as broken glass on a playing field.**

### Rule 6

**Always warm up and cool down properly.**

Sporting injuries can be caused by a fall or a heavy blow; failing to warm up properly, use equipment properly or use the correct technique; or simply by pushing yourself too hard. While injuries are not inevitable, it is very rare for someone involved in physical activity to remain injury-free throughout their life. It is, therefore, sensible to have an awareness of some of the injuries you might experience while playing sport and taking part in physical activity.

The first – and probably the most important – thing to remember is that you should stop if you feel pain. Pain is your body's way of telling you that what you are doing is causing damage. Failing to listen to this warning can make injuries worse and delay recovery.

## Concussion

Concussion is defined by the NHS as "the sudden but short-lived loss of mental function that occurs after a blow or other injury to the head".

The symptoms of concussion are:

- Headaches

- Dizziness

- Nausea/vomiting

- Seeing stars or having blurry vision

- Unconsciousness

- Confusion immediately after the injury

- Temporary loss of memory.

▲ In 2015, George North was forced to take some time out of rugby following concussions.

Concussion is the least serious type of brain injury but could be masking something more serious, like a bleed in the brain or swelling of the brain. Therefore, you should always seek medical help if you receive a blow or other injury to the head.

## Fracture

A fracture is a broken bone. There are two types of fractures:

- An open fracture, where the broken bone penetrates the skin.

- A closed fracture, where the broken bone does not penetrate the skin. The symptoms of a closed fracture include bruising, swelling, deformity and pain, especially if you try to put any weight on the site of injury, and being unable to move the affected part of your body.

You should seek immediate medical attention if you believe you have a fracture.

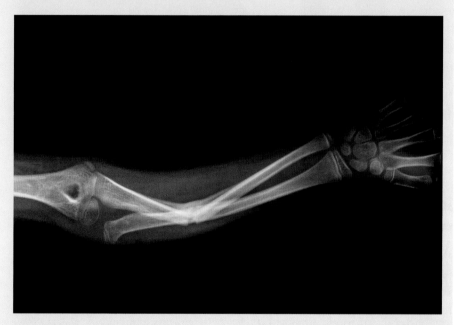

▲ An X-ray of a fractured ulna.

## Dislocation

Bones are dislocated (displaced) at a joint. The symptoms of dislocation include deformity, swelling, bruising, numbness and pain, especially if you try to put any weight on the site of injury, and being unable to move the affected part of your body.

It can be difficult to work out if a bone is broken or dislocated, so it is important to seek medical help at the earliest opportunity.

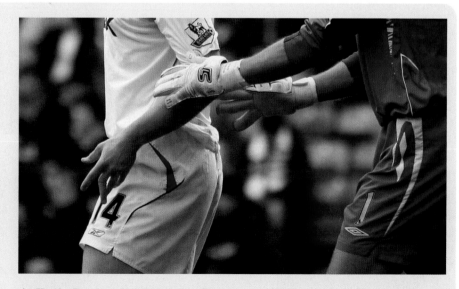

▲ Kevin Davies dislocates his finger.

## Soft tissue injuries

Soft tissue injuries are injuries to the muscles, ligaments and tendons. They include:

▲ Serena Williams suffers a calf strain injury.

- Strain: The muscle or tendon – the connective tissue that attaches muscle to bone – is stretched too much or tears. Symptoms include pain, swelling, bruising, muscle spasms and weakness in the affected area. You can treat most mild strains using the RICE procedure and taking over-the-counter painkillers, but should visit your doctor if the pain and swelling does not subside as expected or the symptoms get worse.

- Tennis elbow: This is an overuse injury, caused by overusing the muscles and tendons attached to your elbow and used to straighten your wrist. It is sometimes, but not always, caused by playing tennis. The main symptom is pain on the outside of your upper forearm, near your elbow, which gets worse when you try to straighten your arm or pick things up. The pain should subside if you rest your elbow, but you should visit your doctor if symptoms persist.

- Golfers elbow: This is an overuse injury, caused by overusing the muscles and tendons attached to your elbow and used to flex your wrist. It is sometimes, but not always, caused by playing golf. The main symptom is pain on the inside of your upper forearm, near your elbow, which gets worse when you try to flex, grip or swing. The pain should subside if you rest your elbow, but you should visit your doctor if symptoms persist.

- Abrasion: Abrasions are caused when a layer of skin is rubbed off. You will feel a hot, burning sensation and your skin will look raw and red. There will be very little bleeding, or none at all. Abrasions should be cleaned and covered by a qualified first-aider.

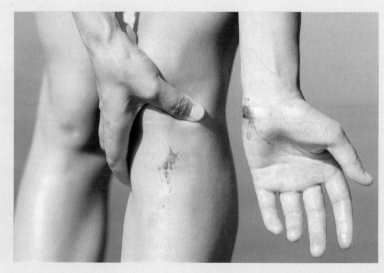

▲ An abrasion.

## Sprain

A sprain happens when the ligament – the connective tissue that attaches bone to bone at joints – is stretched too much or tears. The symptoms of a sprain include pain, swelling, bruising and, if you have a severe sprain, you'll be unable to move the injured joint.

You can treat most mild sprains using the RICE procedure and taking over-the-counter painkillers, but should visit your doctor if the pain and swelling does not subside as expected or the symptoms get worse.

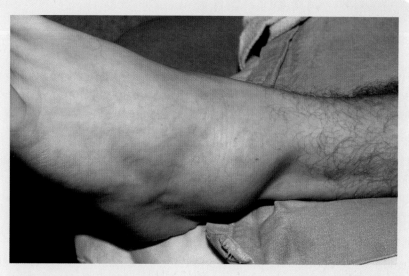

▲ A sprained ankle.

## Torn cartilage

Cartilage is a connective tissue found throughout the body and tearing your cartilage, particularly in your knee joint, is a common injury. Symptoms include pain, swelling, stiffness and a decrease in the range of movement at the affected joint.

You should visit your GP if the symptoms do not subside as expected or the symptoms get worse.

▲ Henrik Larson snaps the ligaments and tears the cartilage in his left knee.

## RICE

The RICE procedure is used to treat strains and sprains.

| | |
|---|---|
| Rest | Rest the injured area. |
| Ice | Apply an ice pack to the injured area. |
| Compression | Apply firm but gentle pressure to the injured area. |
| Elevation | Raise the injured area above the level of the heart. |

## Activity

18 Describe two injuries you have experienced as a result of taking part in sport and physical activity. How were they treated? How long did they take to heal? What, if anything, could you have done to avoid the injury?

The benefits associated with winning – including the adulation and the money from sponsorship and endorsements – drive some performers to cheat. They use performance-enhancing drugs (PEDs) despite the very serious risks.

The use of PEDs has been acknowledged as a problem since the 1960s. In 1981, the International Association of Athletics Federations (IAAF) banned the first athlete for testing positive for anabolic steroids. In 1999, the International Olympic Committee created the World Anti-Doping Agency (WADA) to coordinate the fight against PEDs.

Performers who take PEDs risk losing everything. Not only do they put their health at risk but their reputations and careers can be ruined too. They can be disqualified from competition for the short- to medium-term, or banned for life and stripped of their titles. They will almost certainly lose their sponsorship or endorsement contracts.

▶ **Lance Armstrong was stripped of seven Tour de France victories and banned for life from professional cycling in 2012 for using PEDs. This scandal has tarnished the sport's reputation.**

---

- Increased risk of disease, including liver cancer and organ damage, and increased risk of injury, especially tearing your tendons.
- Increased risk of hair loss and acne.
- Increased risk of high blood pressure.
- Can affect emotional health, increasing aggressive behaviour and depression.
- Increased risk of enlarged breasts in men and facial hair and deep voice in women, and increased risk of infertility.

A man-made copy of the male hormone testosterone, which stimulates muscle growth.

- Faster recovery time.
- Increase in muscle mass, improving performance in sports that need strength, muscular endurance and power.

---

- Increase in aggression
- Increase in heart rate and blood pressure
- Can become addictive

Stimulants are substances that act directly on the central nervous system, speeding up parts of the brain and body.

- Increase in alertness, making a performer able to concentrate better for longer
- Increase in energy, prolonging performance

**—**

- Lowering the heart rate too much can be dangerous. It can lead to heart failure.

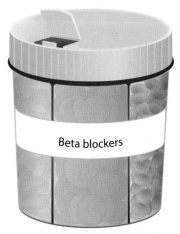

**Beta blockers**

Block the effect of adrenaline and reduce heart rate.

**+**

- Reduction in anxiety allows athletes to stay calm and maintain focus.
- Make a performer's hands steadier, which can be of benefit in sports like snooker, darts, archery and shooting.

---

**—**

- Increased risk of dehydration.
- Increased risk of kidney failure.
- Increased risk of heart failure.
- Increased risk of muscle cramps.
- Increased risk of headaches.
- Increased risk of dizziness.

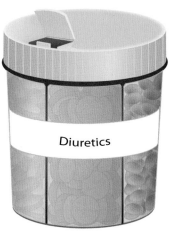

**Diuretics**

Increase the volume of urine removed from the body.

**+**

- Increase in weight loss, which can be of value in sports with weight categories, such as boxing and wrestling.
- Make it difficult to detect other banned substances because traces of the substance in the urine pass out of the body quickly.

---

**—**

- Can effect concentration, balance and coordination.
- Increased pain threshold may lead to further injury.
- Can become addictive.

**Narcotic analgesics (Painkillers)**

Relieve pain.

**+**

- Allow a performer to compete even when they are ill, injured or in pain.

Peptide hormones

- The blood becomes thicker, increasing the risk of heart attack and stroke.

Erythropoietin, known as EPO, is a peptide hormone. It is produced naturally by the kidneys to regulate the production of red blood cells. It can be artificially manufactured and injected.

- The more red blood cells a performer has, the more oxygen is carried to their working muscles. This improves a performer's aerobic capacity. It means they can perform longer before fatigue sets in and their recovery time is shorter.

Growth hormone (GH)

- Increased risk of muscle and joint pain.
- Increased risk of fluid retention, which causes swelling.

GH is produced naturally by the body to stimulate the growth of muscle, cartilage and bone. It can be artificially manufactured and injected.

- Increase in muscle size and mass, leading to an increase in strength.
- Increase in metabolic rate, which helps the body to burn more fat.
- Speeds up recovery from muscle fatigue and injury.

Blood doping

- High risk of kidney failure.
- High risk of blood borne infections, such as HIV, hepatitis B and hepatitis C.
- Increased risk of blood clots.
- Increased risk of an allergic reaction.

Injecting oxygenated blood.

- More oxygen is transported to the working muscles, increasing endurance and allowing the performer to train for longer.

## Activity

**19** The World Anti-Doping Agency (WADA) monitors anti-doping policies in all sports around the world, researches PEDs to try and stay one step ahead of the cheats, and is involved in education. You have been asked by WADA to prepare a video advert about a PED of your choice. Your advert should acknowledge why a performer might consider taking the PED, but should emphasise the negative effects on sporting performance and the performer's lifestyle.

It is important to warm up before you take part in sport and physical activity, including training sessions, and to cool down afterwards.

## Warming up

A warm-up prepares your mind and body for the work ahead, improving performance and preventing injury. It gradually increases the volume and speed with which oxygen is delivered to the working muscles, so your body is working efficiently by the time you begin the main activity. It also warms up your muscles to limit the risk of sprains and strains, and your joints to allow a full range of movement. A warm-up should last a minimum of ten minutes.

There are four stages to a warm-up:

### Stage 1: Pulse raising

Gradually raising the heart rate to increase blood flow around the body and speed up oxygen delivery to the working muscles by performing exercises that make you breathe faster such as jogging, cycling, swimming or rowing.

Examples of pulse-raising activities include:

- Eight-station circuit, including exercises like rope jumping, star jumps, shuttle runs and burpees

- Aerobic dance

- Jogging around a football pitch while dribbling a football.

### Stage 2: Stretching and joint mobilisation

Stretching the muscles and mobilising the joints that will be used during the main activity. The type of stretching you do will depend on the sport or physical activity for which you are preparing your body.

**Exam tip**

If you feel warm towards the end of your warm-up, and need to take a layer of clothing off, it is a good indicator that your muscles and joints are ready to start the main activity.

**Activity**

20 Prepare a warm-up for a sport you take part in regularly, remembering to include a pulse-raising exercise, stretching and joint mobilisation exercises, sport specific drills and a psychological warm-up. Lead others through your warm-up.

▲ Footballers perform dynamic stretches, like lateral lunges, and joint mobilisation exercises before a match.

### Stage 3: Sport specific drills

Practising the skills and techniques needed during training or competition prepares the performer's body for the movements they will need to perform. For example, a sprinter will perform butt kicks, bounding, high knees and skipping.

### Stage 4: Psychological warm-up

Good mental preparation during a warm-up ensures that all of a performer's attention is totally focused on the performance and nothing is able to distract from the task at hand. See page 152–3 for more on psychological warm-ups.

## Cooling down

A cool down reduces your heart rate and your rate of breathing back to their resting rates. It helps remove the waste products, including lactic acid, that have built up in your muscles during the main activity, limiting soreness after exercise. It also improves flexibility and prevents blood pooling.

Blood pooling occurs when blood collects around the muscles in your legs. It reduces blood flow and oxygen to the brain and makes you feel dizzy and nauseous.

There are three stages to a cool down:

### Stage 1: Pulse lowering

Reducing the heart rate and rate of breathing by performing light exercises for a minimum of five minutes or until your heart rate has returned to normal.

Examples of pulse-lowering activities include jogging, cycling or swimming slowly.

### Stage 2: Active static stretching

Lengthening and relaxing the muscles used during the main activity by holding them for 10–30 seconds. There should be some discomfort but no pain.

▲ A hurdler performs a static stretch, holding the stretch in a challenging but comfortable position mimicking the hurdle position.

**Exam tip**

If you feel dizzy, nauseous or worn out after exercise, it is a good indication that you have not done a proper cool down.

Examples of the most common active static stretches:

## Stage 3: Developmental stretching

Improving flexibility and increasing the range of movement at the joint by lengthening the muscles used during the main activity. Each stretch should be held for 30–60 seconds.

There are two types of stretches that will improve and increase flexibility.

- Active static stretches, held for 30–60 seconds.

- Passive static stretches, held for 30–60 seconds.

Passive stretches involve some form of assistance to help you achieve a greater stretch. This assistance could be your body weight, a strap, gravity or another person. You need to relax the muscle that is being stretched and rely on the external force to hold you in place. For example:

▲ Passive stretching: tension bands are used to stretch the hamstrings and gastrocnemius muscles.

▲ Passive stretching: a stool is used to stretch the quadriceps and hamstrings muscles.

# Exam-style questions

1 Reggie is a 17-year-old footballer. He has just taken the 30 m sprint test.

**Table 1** shows the normative data for 16–19-year-olds for the 30 m sprint test.

| | Excellent | Above average | Average | Below average | Poor |
|---|---|---|---|---|---|
| **Male** | < 4 sec | 4.2–4 sec | 4.4–4.3 sec | 4.6–4.5 sec | > 4.6 sec |
| **Female** | < 4.5 sec | 4.6–4.5 sec | 4.8–4.7 sec | 5–4.9 sec | > 5 sec |

*Source: Davis, B. et al., Physical Education and the Study of Sport, 4th edition, Harcourt, 2000.*

Which one of the following is the correct rating for Reggie, given his score of 4.08 in the 30 m sprint test? (1)
- **A** Excellent
- **B** Above average
- **C** Average
- **D** Below average

2 Which one of the following performance-enhancing drugs is a performer most likely to take to increase production of red blood cells? (1)
- **A** Diuretics
- **B** Narcotic analgesics
- **C** EPO
- **D** GH

3 Which one of the following fitness tests measures strength? (1)
- **A** Sit and reach test
- **B** Vertical jump test
- **C** Cooper 12-minute test
- **D** Grip dynamometer

4 Which one of the following is **not** an example of a training method that can be used for improving cardiovascular fitness? (1)
- **A** Continuous training
- **B** Weight training
- **C** Fartlek training
- **D** Interval training

5 A 50 m sprint swimmer wants to improve her time in a race and her coach has included weight training in her training programme to help her do this.
- **a)** State two advantages of using weight training to improve fitness. (2)
- **b)** Using the FITT principle, state how the swimmer's coach would apply intensity to the weight training programme in order to increase fitness levels. (2)

6 Explain two reasons why qualitative data from a PARQ can be used to plan a Personal Exercise Programme (PEP). (4)

7 Cardiovascular fitness (aerobic endurance) and strength are components of fitness.
Explain the importance of each of these components of fitness to a netball player. (4)

8 Explain **one** disadvantage for an athlete of using diuretics. (2)

9 Evaluate whether or not an elite cyclist who wants to compete in the Tour de France should use a combination of Fartlek training and continuous training. (9)

10 Using examples, evaluate the importance of using the principles of training when planning a PEP to improve a football player's fitness levels and performance. (9)

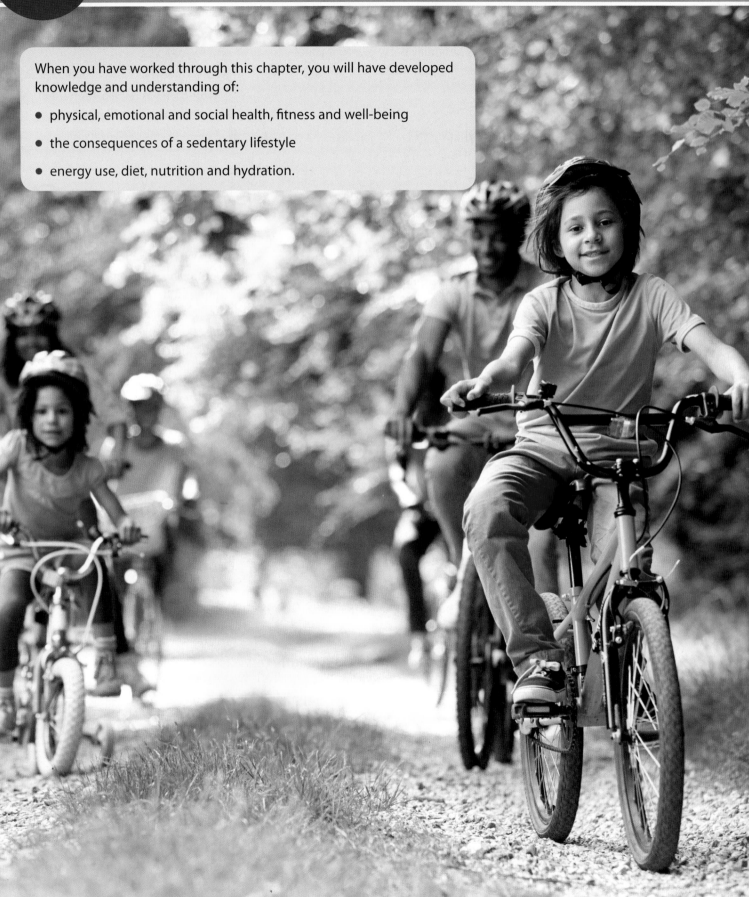

# 4 Health, fitness and well-being

When you have worked through this chapter, you will have developed knowledge and understanding of:

- physical, emotional and social health, fitness and well-being
- the consequences of a sedentary lifestyle
- energy use, diet, nutrition and hydration.

A person with high levels of **well-being** is generally happier, more successful and better able to cope with difficult circumstances than a person with lower levels of well-being.

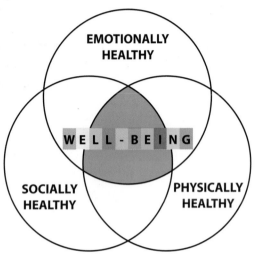

▲ Good physical, emotional and social health are all essential for well-being.

## Physical health

Taking part in more physical activity and developing your components of fitness will improve your physical health.

**Cardiovascular endurance:** Improving your cardiovascular endurance means you will be able to work harder for longer, and burn more calories. You will feel like you have more energy and you will find it easier to lose weight or maintain your optimum weight. Your risk of developing diseases, such as heart disease, high blood pressure and type 2 diabetes, is significantly reduced, while your immune system's ability to fight off disease is increased. You will also find that you get to sleep faster at night, and get better quality sleep.

**Strength:** Your muscles will become bigger and stronger, which means you will burn more calories when you are at rest. Your ligaments and tendons will also become stronger, reducing your risk of injury. Daily activities will become easier as you become stronger.

**Flexibility:** Increasing the flexibility of your soft tissues – your muscles, ligaments and tendons – makes daily activities easier and helps prevent or limit the severity of injuries caused by falls and other accidents. It also increases the blood supply to your muscles, helping you to recover more quickly from physical activity and injuries, and reducing tension in your muscles making you feel more relaxed.

**Muscular endurance:** Increasing your muscular endurance increases the blood supply to your working muscles, delivering more oxygen and eliminating waste products more quickly. You will be able to work harder for longer, and burn more calories. You will feel like you have more energy, find it easier to lose weight or maintain your optimum weight, and will reduce your risk of injury.

**Body composition:** Taking part in physical activity reduces your body fat and increases your lean muscle mass. This will increase your self-esteem and reduce your risk of developing diseases linked to high levels of body fat, such as heart disease, high blood pressure and type 2 diabetes.

**Components of fitness**

**Agility:** Improving your agility can help you move quickly and fluidly, which can be helpful if you have to dodge out of the way of something.

**Coordination:** Improving your coordination makes many daily activities that involve using different parts of your body together smoothly and efficiently easier, including cooking and playing computer games, and reduces your risk of injury.

**Reaction time:** Improving your reaction time will mean you will be able to respond to stimuli faster, which will help you in all aspects of your daily life. For example, you will be better at reacting to danger.

**Balance:** Improving your balance makes tasks such as climbing ladders and reaching for high objects easier, and reduces your risk of falls.

**Power:** Improving your physical power can help you in dangerous situations, enabling you to push heavy objects out of the way quickly and pull someone out of danger.

**Speed:** Improving your speed will help you do things faster, including getting to places more quickly and moving away from dangerous situations.

## Emotional health

People who are emotionally or "psychologically" healthy are happy, self-confident, self-aware and resilient. They understand their emotions and are in control of their behaviour. They are able to cope well with both positive and negative criticism and with change, and are able to bounce back when life gets challenging.

Participation in physical activity and sport helps develop and maintain emotional health, because:

- exercising releases hormones called endorphins, which make you feel happier and more relaxed, and less stressed and anxious

- you will have more energy if you exercise, making you feel better able to cope with the physical demands of a busy life

- feeling physically healthier boosts your self-esteem and makes you a more confident person

- as you get older, exercising also stimulates the growth of new brain cells, reducing the risk of age-related diseases such as dementia.

## Social health

Socially healthy people are able to form and maintain good relationships with others. This does not mean they never have disagreements, but they are able to communicate effectively with others to avoid or resolve disputes. A socially healthy person is also sensitive to the needs of the people around them and can adapt to different social situations.

Taking part in physical activity and sport can improve your social health. You will meet new people, often from different social backgrounds, and make new friends. Being part of a team or a club can give you a sense of belonging, as you all work together to achieve a common goal, and you will develop your teamwork skills.

# How to achieve well-being through physical activity and sport

The NHS provides guidelines for the amount of physical activity people of different ages need to do each week to stay healthy or to improve their health.

## 5 to 18-year-olds

Behaviour learned when you are young often carries through into later life, so a physically active child will often grow up to become a physically active adult.

To maintain a basic level of health, children and young people aged 5 to 18 need to do:

- At least 60 minutes of physical activity every day, which should range between moderate activity, such as cycling and playground activities, and vigorous activity, such as running and tennis.

- On three days a week, these activities should involve exercises for strong muscles, such as push-ups, and exercises for strong bones, such as jumping and running.

Many vigorous activities can help you build strong muscles and bones, such as anything involving running and jumping, like gymnastics, martial arts and football.

Children and young people should reduce the time they spend sitting watching TV, playing computer games and travelling by car when they could walk or cycle instead.

*Source: www.nhs.uk/Livewell/fitness/Pages/physical-activity-guidelines-for-young-people.aspx*

## 19 to 64-year-olds

To stay healthy, adults aged 19 to 64 should try to be active daily and should do:

- At least 150 minutes of moderate aerobic activity, such as cycling or fast walking every week

**and**

- Strength exercises on two or more days a week that work all the major muscles (legs, hips, back, abdomen, chest, shoulders and arms)

**OR**

- 75 minutes of vigorous aerobic activity, such as running or a game of singles tennis every week

**and**

- Strength exercises on two or more days a week that work all the major muscles (legs, hips, back, abdomen, chest, shoulders and arms)

**OR**

- A mix of moderate and vigorous aerobic activity every week. For example, two 30-minute runs plus 30 minutes of fast walking equates to 150 minutes of moderate aerobic activity

**and**

- Strength exercises on two or more days a week that work all the major muscles (legs, hips, back, abdomen, chest, shoulders and arms).

All adults should also break up long periods of sitting with light activity.

*Source: www.nhs.uk/Livewell/fitness/Pages/physical-activity-guidelines-for-adults.aspx*

## 65-year-olds and over

Adults aged 65 or older, who are generally fit and have no health conditions that limit their mobility, should try and keep active every day and should do:

- At least 150 minutes of moderate aerobic activity such as cycling or walking every week

**and**

- Strength exercises on two or more days a week that work all the major muscles (legs, hips, back, abdomen, chest, shoulders and arms)

**OR**

- 75 minutes of vigorous aerobic activity, such as running or a game of singles tennis every week

**and**

- Strength exercises on two or more days a week that work all the major muscles (legs, hips, back, abdomen, chest, shoulders and arms)

**OR**

- A mix of moderate and vigorous aerobic activity every week. For example, two 30-minute runs plus 30 minutes of fast walking equates to 150 minutes of moderate aerobic activity

**and**

- Strength exercises on two or more days a week that work all the major muscles (legs, hips, back, abdomen, chest, shoulders and arms).

All adults should also break up long periods of sitting with light activity.

Older adults at risk of falls, such as people with weak legs, poor balance and some medical conditions, should do exercises to improve balance and coordination on at least two days a week. Examples include yoga, tai chi and dancing.

*Source: www.nhs.uk/Livewell/fitness/Pages/physical-activity-guidelines-for-older-adults.aspx*

Both **quantitative** and **qualitative data** can be collected using a questionnaire. Quantitative data is usually collected using closed questions. These are questions that have a defined answer. An example of a closed question is:

How often do you exercise?

- More than twice a week
- Once a week
- Twice a week
- Less than once a week

If you ask enough people closed questions you will have data you can present in a table, graph or pie chart.

Qualitative data is usually collected using open questions. These are unstructured questions that gather a wide range of information about how the person completing the questionnaire feels, thinks and behaves. Examples of open questions include:

- How do you feel, physically, just after you have exercised?
- What effect has taking part in sport and physical activity had on your self-esteem?
- Has taking part in sport and physical activity changed your relationships with other people?

It is much harder to present, interpret and analyse qualitative data. Often researchers read completed questionnaires carefully and tease out trends. A trend is information that is being repeated by more than one of the people who completed the questionnaires and that can be used to describe the general direction in which something is developing at any given moment. Analysing trends in quantitative data allows you to make predictions about what people who didn't complete your questionnaire might think or feel about the issues you are investigating.

## Key terms

**Quantitative data:** Data that focuses on measuring things; it involves numbers.

**Qualitative data:** Data that focuses on understanding things; it involves detailed information about the way people think and behave.

### Activity

1. Find out how participation in physical activity and sport improves physical, emotional and social health by creating a questionnaire to collect qualitative data.

   a) Think about what you want to find out and write your questionnaire. It should contain no more than ten questions. Begin with a couple of closed questions to establish the age of the person completing the questionnaire and how often they exercise and then move on to open questions.

   b) Ask at least six people of more or less the same age to complete your questionnaire.

   c) Interpret the data collected. What trends can you spot?

   d) Analyse the data collected. How do the trends you spotted influence your thinking about the way in which participation in physical activity and sport improves physical, emotional and social health?

**Fitness** is the ability to meet the demands of the environment. There is, therefore, a close relationship between well-being and fitness because if you are fit you are physically healthy. Being fit also contributes to your emotional and social well-being.

### Key term

**Fitness:** The ability to meet the demands of the environment.

**The positive health effects of being fit:**

- you can maintain your optimum weight
- your risk of developing diseases such as heart disease, high blood pressure and type 2 diabetes is reduced
- your cardio-respiratory system works efficiently so you are able to perform daily tasks quickly and easily
- you feel happier and more confident, with a more positive body image
- you fall asleep faster and get better quality sleep
- you are able to recover from exercise, illness and injury more quickly.

### Activity

2 Write a rap or a song with the title "Fitness: positive and negative effects" and perform it for the class. Feeling shy? Video it!

**Done properly, there are very few negative health effects of being fit, but there are some things to watch out for:**

- exercising can become addictive, which leads to overtraining

- focusing too much on body shape can cause body dysmorphic disorder, in which a person has a distorted view of how they look. For example, they might worry that their legs are too skinny or their abs are not visible enough, causing them to overtrain

- too much training can damage the joints and cause overuse injuries, such as tennis elbow and golfers elbow. In the long term, it can also cause health conditions such as osteoarthritis (where the joints become stiff and painful) or osteoporosis (where the bones become brittle and fragile)

- training too much and not giving your body enough time to rest and recover between training sessions can lead to an increase in soft tissue injuries because your soft tissues are not given enough time to repair properly.

## The importance of a well-designed Personal Exercise Programme (PEP)

A well-designed PEP can help you harness all the positive health effects of being fit and avoid all the negative health effects. There are four stages to a PEP, which are discussed in more detail in Chapter 7:

1. Designing a PEP: To ensure you gain the maximum health benefits from a PEP it is critical that it is designed to meet your individual needs.
2. Carrying out a PEP: You have to stick to your PEP for it to work. You have to be in it to win it!
3. Monitoring a PEP: It's helpful to monitor your PEP as you go, so that you can make small changes, if you miss a training session or the facilities or equipment you have access to changes, for example. This ensures you achieve your goals.
4. Evaluating a PEP: When you have completed a PEP it is valuable to consider the progress you have made and to use this information to help you develop your next PEP. This ensures you continue to benefit from the positive health effects of being fit because, as you know, the principle of reversibility means that any adaptations to your body will reverse if you stop training.

We all make **lifestyle choices** about what we eat, how much physical activity we do, the balance of work, rest and sleep in our lives and whether or not we drink alcohol and smoke. Some of the choices we make will have a positive influence on our health, fitness and well-being; other choices will have a more negative impact.

> ### Key term
>
> **Lifestyle choices:** The choices we make about how we live and behave that impact on our health.

## Diet

### Eating a healthy diet:
- boosts your energy levels, so you are better able to enjoy life
- will supply your body with the essential nutrients it needs for a healthy immune system, helping you fight off illnesses
- reduces the risk of developing serious health conditions, such as heart disease, type 2 diabetes, high blood pressure, high cholesterol or stroke
- can reduce your stress levels and improve your sleep patterns
- will help you lose weight, if you are currently overweight, or maintain a healthy weight.

### Eating an unhealthy diet:
- leads to deficiencies in essential nutrients and causes health conditions, such as osteoporosis and rickets, as well as fatigue and muscle weakness
- leads to an increase in weight and body fat, which puts you at risk of developing health conditions, such as heart disease, type 2 diabetes, high blood pressure, high cholesterol and stroke
- can affect your concentration levels and make you feel lethargic, making it more difficult to find the energy to exercise
- can affect your quality of sleep
- can cause you to feel guilty and depressed, especially if you overeat.

# Activity levels

**Living an inactive life:**

- increases your risk of disease

- increases your risk of low-self esteem, anxiety and depression

- decreases your muscle mass, overall strength and energy levels, making daily tasks such as carrying shopping bags more difficult.

**Living an active life:**

- lowers your risk of disease

- lowers your risk of developing mental-health conditions, such as depression or dementia

- boosts your self-esteem, the quality of your sleep, and your energy levels

- reduces stress and anxiety

- improves your fitness levels.

## Work/rest/sleep balance

When your life is balanced, you work hard but you also have enough time to rest and to sleep. Work includes schoolwork, employment and sport and physical activity. Rest might involve chatting to your friends on social media or listening to music. Sleep is also important because your mind and body have time to recover from the demands of the day while you are asleep. For example, the body releases human growth hormone while you are asleep, which helps soft tissues repair and boosts muscle mass.

**A good work/rest/sleep balance:**

- improves your physical, emotional and social health

- makes you feel more in control of your life, helping to reduce stress and making you more effective in all areas of your life. You are more productive at work, are better at making good decisions and form stronger and longer-lasting relationships.

**A poor work/rest/sleep balance can:**

- increase your risk of depression

- lead to weight gain

- increase your risk of illness and disease, including your risk of high blood pressure and heart disease

- increase stress and anxiety

- lead to drinking more alcohol and smoking more cigarettes

- result in poor-quality sleep.

## Recreational drugs

Recreational drugs are drugs that are taken for pleasure rather than for medical reasons. Many recreational drugs, such as heroin and cocaine, are illegal. Others, such as alcohol and nicotine, are legal to consume if you are over a certain age. However, just because a drug is legal does not mean it is good for you. Drinking alcohol and smoking can have a negative effect on your health.

### Alcohol

Consuming alcohol:

- can lead to dehydration because alcohol is a diuretic. It makes the kidneys produce more urine and reduces the amount of water in your body, upsetting the delicate balance of minerals and affecting the way your body functions

- reduces your cardiovascular fitness and muscular endurance. While it focuses on breaking down the alcohol you have drunk, the liver cannot produce as much glucose as it would normally. Glucose is used as a fuel in energy production, so less glucose means that you will have less energy

- makes the nerve cells in your brain less excited and slows them down. This in turn affects many things, including your coordination, concentration and reaction time

- can lead to weight gain because alcohol is high in sugar and calories

- disrupts sleep pattern, decreasing the release of human growth hormone and slowing the body's ability to heal itself

- can lead to liver damage and mental-health conditions, such as addiction, depression and, in the long term, memory loss.

## Nicotine

▲ The lung on the left is from a non-smoker. The darker, rougher and misshapen lung on the right is from a smoker.

Smoking:

- makes you feel tired faster. When you smoke a cigarette your cardiovascular and respiratory systems are unable to work efficiently, and they are unable to carry as much oxygen around the body as they normally would. This is because nicotine constricts the blood vessels and the carbon monoxide in the smoke makes it more difficult for the already limited supply of blood to carry oxygen

- increases your risk of disease, including lung cancer, bronchitis, pneumonia and emphysema

- leads to addiction. Nicotine is a highly addictive drug and regular smokers find it very difficult to stop

- causes harm to those around you, who breathe in the smoke by passive smoking.

E-cigarettes have become popular in the UK since smoking was banned in enclosed public places and workplaces in 2007. E-cigarettes are viewed as safer than cigarettes because their vapour contains fewer of the harmful chemicals, such as carbon monoxide, contained in cigarette smoke. However, e-cigarettes still contain nicotine and the long-term effects on people who smoke them, and those around them, is not yet known.

**Activity**

3   Design an information leaflet for a Year 9 Personal, Social and Health Education workshop on the positive and negative impacts of a person's lifestyle choices on health, fitness and well-being. Remember to include photos to illustrate the points you are making and provide websites where the reader can find further information.

There are serious consequences to leading a **sedentary lifestyle**. You can become overweight, overfat or obese.

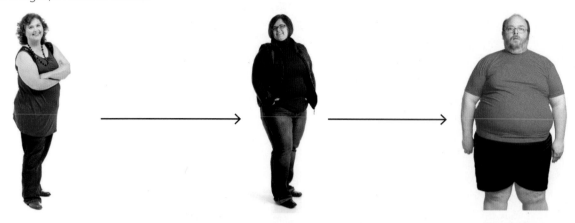

▲ A person is **overweight** if they weigh more than the ideal weight for their height.

▲ A person is **overfat** if they have more than the ideal amount of body fat.

▲ A person is **obese** if they weigh significantly more than the ideal weight for their height and have an excess amount of body fat.

## Activity  DATA

**4** This graph shows the percentage of children who are overweight, by age group, between 1994 and 2013.

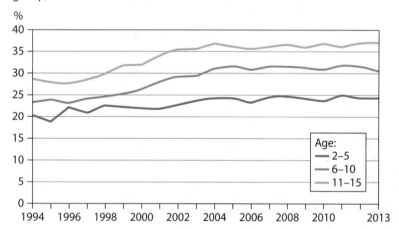

Source: King's College London, from www.bbc.co.uk/news/health-31041864

**a)** Interpret the data: Describe the trend for each year group between 1994 and 2013.

**b)** Analyse the data: What does the trend suggest about how the lifestyles of 2 to 5-year-olds have changed between 2003 and 2013?

**c)** Analyse the data: Predict the percentage of children who will be overweight, by age group, in 2020.

## Key terms

**Sedentary lifestyle:** A lifestyle where there is little, irregular or no physical activity.

**Overweight:** Weighing more than the ideal weight for your height.

**Overfat:** Having more than the ideal amount of body fat.

**Obese:** Weighing significantly more than the ideal weight for your height and having an excess amount of body fat.

## Exam tip  DATA

A trend is a direction of movement. It describes the general direction in which something is developing at any given moment. Analysing trends in quantitative data allows you make predictions about what will happen in the future.

Body Mass Index (BMI) is a way of calculating whether or not you are an ideal weight. This BMI chart can be used as a guide to determine whether or not an adult is underweight, overweight, obese or very obese. The NHS provides a "healthy weight calculator" to help parents determine if their children are a healthy weight.

When thinking about healthy weight, it is important to remember that muscle weighs more than fat. BMI charts do not take into account how much of your body is made up of muscle. This means that a rugby player or a weightlifter would be considered overweight based on their BMI. This is because their high percentage of muscle means they have a heavy weight, but they are not unhealthy. As a result, elite performers tend not to use BMI as a method for calculating their optimum weight.

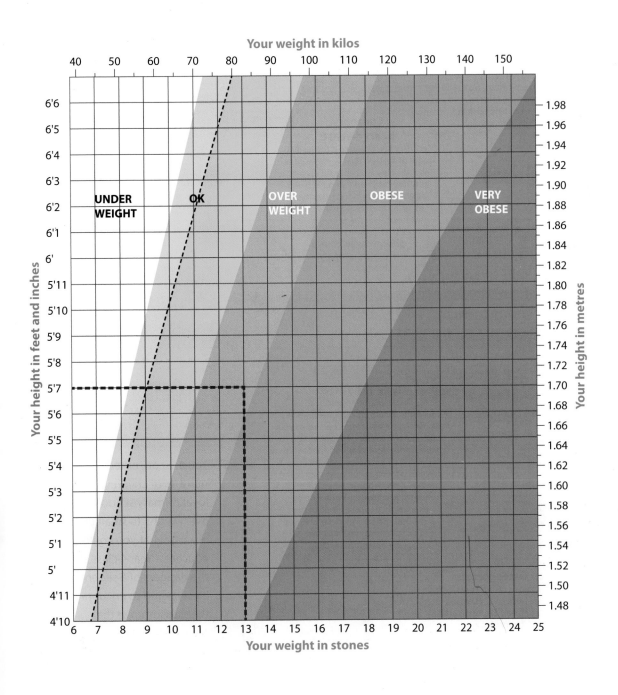

# Long-term health problems

Living a sedentary lifestyle increases your risk of long-term health problems.

**Poor posture**
Spending a lot of your time sitting still can lead to poor posture. And, when your body is constantly held in unnatural positions, it can lead to back pain and joint pain. Exercising can improve your posture.

**High blood pressure**
If your blood pressure is often high then this puts extra strain on your heart and blood vessels. Eventually, if left unchecked, high blood pressure can lead to a heart attack or a stroke. Exercise can help lower blood pressure.

**Depression**
Depression is a mental illness that ranges from mild depression, when you feel low and everything feels like a lot of effort, to clinical depression, which can be life-threatening as it is often accompanied by suicidal thoughts. Exercising releases hormones called endorphins, which make you feel happier and more relaxed and can help combat depression.

**Impact on components of fitness**
Leading a sedentary lifestyle has a negative impact on all eleven components of fitness. It can reduce your cardiovascular fitness, your strength, your muscular endurance, your flexibility, your body composition, your agility, your balance, your coordination, your power, your reaction time and your speed.

**Coronary heart disease**
Coronary heart disease is the leading cause of death in the UK. The walls of the coronary arteries build up with fatty deposits, narrowing the blood vessels that carry blood to the heart, reducing the oxygen received by the heart. Exercise helps remove the fatty deposits and helps prevent the build up of more fatty deposits.

**You are more likely to suffer from these long-term health problems if you live a sedentary lifestyle**

**Loss of muscle tone**
If you live a sedentary lifestyle and don't move very much you will lose muscle mass. You will become weaker and it will become harder to complete daily tasks. Exercise increases muscle mass.

**Type 2 diabetes**
Insulin is a hormone produced by your body to convert carbohydrates into glucose. Type 2 diabetes occurs when your body doesn't produce enough insulin to function properly or your body doesn't react correctly to the insulin produced. Type 2 diabetes is far more common than type 1 diabetes, which occurs when the body doesn't produce any insulin. Being overweight or obese is one of the causes of type 2 diabetes and exercise helps you maintain your optimum weight.

**Osteoporosis**
Osteoporosis causes your bones to become weak and brittle, and more likely to break. Exercise increases bone density.

## Activity

5   You are concerned about the number of children in your local primary school who are overweight. In small groups, discuss what you could do to educate a Year 4 class about the dangers of a sedentary lifestyle and to encourage them to improve their physical health.

Eating a balanced diet is an essential part of a healthy lifestyle, and the "eatwell plate" has been developed by the government to inform people of the proportions of different food groups they should eat in order to have a balanced diet. Eating a balanced diet guarantees that you will consume the right proportion of all seven components of a healthy, balanced diet: carbohydrates, proteins, fats, vitamins, minerals, fibre and water.

## The eatwell plate

Use the eatwell plate to help you get the balance right. It shows how much of what you eat should come from each food group.

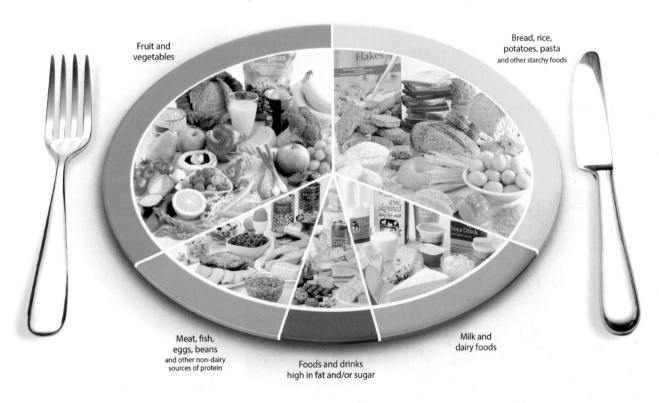

Fruit and vegetables

Bread, rice, potatoes, pasta and other starchy foods

Meat, fish, eggs, beans and other non-dairy sources of protein

Foods and drinks high in fat and/or sugar

Milk and dairy foods

Public Health England in association with the Welsh Government, the Scottish Government and the Food Standards Agency in Northern Ireland

Everyone who takes part in physical activity and sport should eat a balanced diet to ensure their bodies are prepared to cope with the demands placed on them. But, as we shall see, some performers have slightly different dietary requirements in order that their bodies can perform at their very best.

## The role of macronutrients in physical activity and sport

**Macronutrients** are the nutrients that you need to consume in relatively large amounts in order to eat a balanced diet. "Macro" means "large scale".

### Key term

**Macronutrients:** Nutrients that you need to consume in relatively large amounts in order to eat a balanced diet. These are carbohydrates, proteins and fats.

## Carbohydrates

Carbohydrates are the main source of energy for the body. They are stored in the body as glycogen and, when we exercise, glycogen is broken down into glucose, which provides the working muscles with energy. When supplies of glucose become depleted, less energy is produced and the performer becomes fatigued. It is critical that someone taking part in physical activity and sport eats enough carbohydrates:

- 50–60% of a non-performer's diet should consist of carbohydrates

- 60–70% of a performer's diet should consist of carbohydrates, because a performer needs more energy than a non-performer.

There are two types of carbohydrates:

**1)** Simple sugars: These break down quickly and provide a burst of energy.

**2)** Complex starches: These break down slowly and release energy slowly, making them an ideal source of energy for performers.

The body can use carbohydrates or fats to produce aerobic energy, but it needs more oxygen to convert fats into energy than it does to convert carbohydrates into energy. Endurance athletes therefore use a strategy called **carbohydrate loading** to boost their performance. They increase the amount of carbohydrates eaten a few days before a competition in order to maximise the amount of carbohydrates stored in the body as glycogen. This means they can sustain an increased level of physical activity for longer.

▲ Examples of simple sugars include table sugar, honey, sweets, fruit juice, milk, sugar, chocolate, yogurt and jam.

▲ Examples of complex starches include vegetables, bread, pasta, rice and oatmeal.

### Key term

**Carbohydrate loading:** A strategy used by endurance athletes to boost glycogen stores before a competition.

◄ Evidence suggests that maximizing glycogen stores through carbohydrate loading can improve the finish time of someone aiming to complete a marathon in 4 hours by up to 7 minutes.

## Proteins

Protein provides the body with amino acids. These are the building blocks of all human cells, controlling many vital processes, and are essential for muscle growth and repair as well as a healthy immune system.

Power athletes require a higher intake of protein than endurance athletes. The general rule of thumb is that endurance athletes should eat 1.2 grams of protein per kilogram of body weight, while strength and power athletes should eat 1.2 to 1.7 grams of protein per kilogram of body weight.

The timing of protein intake is particularly important for power athletes. Muscles adapt to exercise by increasing in size and becoming stronger because of a process called hypertrophy (see page 90). Small tears appear in the muscles during training and, when these heal, the muscles grow back thicker. Power athletes, who are training to increase their strength and speed, will create a lot of these small tears. It is, therefore, important that they consume enough protein after training to help their bodies repair quickly and build muscle.

▲ Good sources of protein include meat, fish and shellfish, eggs, pulses, beans and nuts.

◄ Appropriately timed protein plays an important part in a performer's training programme because it is essential for proper recovery and muscle growth.

## Fats

Fats are an essential part of a healthy diet. Consuming fats doesn't make you fat; it's consuming more calories than you burn off that will make you gain weight (see page 131). Fats are an important source of energy. They are also important for transporting fat-soluble vitamins around the body and certain fatty acids are vital for good health.

There are two main types of fats:

- saturated fats are typically solid at room temperature. Too much saturated fat in your diet increases your risk of developing heart disease, so you should limit your consumption of foods containing saturated fats

- unsaturated fats are normally liquid at room temperature. They are much healthier than saturated fats and play a role in reducing your risk of developing heart disease.

You need more oxygen to convert fatty acids into energy, which means you have to run at a slower pace to allow your cardiovascular system time to deliver enough oxygen to the working muscles.

▲ Saturated fat is found in fatty meat, butter, cheese, cakes, crisps and biscuits.

▲ Unsaturated fat is found in oily fish, nuts, olive oil, sunflower oil and avocados.

## The role of micronutrients in physical activity and sport

**Micronutrients** are the nutrients that you need to consume in relatively small amounts in order to eat a balanced diet. "Micro" means "small scale".

### Key term

**Micronutrients:** Nutrients that you need to consume in relatively small amounts in order to eat a balanced diet. These include vitamins and minerals.

## Vitamins

Vitamins play an important role in ensuring vital chemical reactions take part in the body. For example, Vitamins B3 and B6 help gaseous exchange to take place. Vitamins are also responsible for making sure that essential bodily functions take place, including blood production and hormone regulation.

▲ Vitamins can be found in fruits, vegetables, dairy products, oily fish, beans, seeds and nuts.

There are 13 essential vitamins, in two groups:

- fat-soluble vitamins, which are stored in fatty tissue and called on when needed: Vitamin A, Vitamin D, Vitamin E, Vitamin K and Beta-carotene

- water-soluble vitamins, which generally cannot be stored and must be replenished every day: Vitamin C, the six B vitamins, Biotin and Folic acid.

◄ Vitamin D is important for healthy bones, which all performers need. Your body produces it when your skin is exposed to sunlight. There are also a few foods, such as eggs, that naturally contain Vitamin D. Performers who mostly train inside, such as figure skaters, can be deficient in this vital vitamin unless they eat foods that are fortified with Vitamin D or take vitamin supplements.

## Minerals

Minerals play an essential role in almost all bodily functions. To function properly, the body needs a wide range of minerals, including calcium, fluoride, iron, magnesium, phosphorous and potassium. For example, calcium is found in strong, healthy bones and iron plays an important part in energy production.

◀ Minerals, including potassium, sodium and chloride, can be lost if you sweat a lot during a long or intense period of physical activity. Sports drinks containing electrolytes can help replenish these losses.

▶ Minerals are found in many foods. For example, shellfish, almonds and watercress are all good dietary sources of iron.

### Activity

6   Research two vitamins and two minerals and prepare a fact sheet about each of them. For each micronutrient, identify foods in which it can be found and explain:

- what it does

- why it is important for a performer to include it in their diet

- at least one health condition that can develop if you do not have enough of it in your diet and how it could affect performance in physical activity and sport.

## Water and the importance of maintaining hydration during physical activity and sport

Water makes up 60 per cent of our bodyweight and plays a crucial part in ensuring our bodies function effectively. Water:

- carries nutrients around the body

- keeps the joints lubricated

- helps remove waste products through urine

- regulates body temperature through sweating.

You can get your water intake from a variety of sources, including fruit juice, milk, fizzy drinks, coffee and tea, but drinking water is the best way to maintain adequate levels of **hydration**. Fruit and vegetables such as oranges and cucumbers that are high in moisture can also help with hydration.

When you are fully hydrated, your body contains the amount of water in its cells, tissues and organs needed to function correctly. If you do not have enough water in your body you are "dehydrated". Symptoms of mild dehydration include thirst, dark-coloured urine, a head rush, a headache and flushed skin, and means

### Key term

Hydration: Being hydrated means your body contains the correct amount of water in its cells, tissues and organs to function correctly. If you do not have enough water in your body you are "dehydrated".

that your body is not performing at its optimum level. Minor dehydration can also affect your ability to concentrate, which can have a negative effect on your performance. Severe dehydration is very serious as it can lead to death.

The average recommended daily intake of water is 2.5 litres of water for men and 2 litres for women; more if you are taking part in physical activity and sport or in hot weather. Exactly how much extra water you need before, during and after exercise to ensure you are fully hydrated depends on the intensity and duration of the exercise. Factors such as air temperature, humidity, altitude and your body composition also affect how much water you need during exercise.

As a rule of thumb, drink small amounts of water regularly throughout the day. Don't wait until you are thirsty because you are probably already a little dehydrated by that time.

▲ Sports drinks help you hydrate after high intensity physical activity, but water is sufficient for most people after a training or physical activity session lasting less than 60 minutes, or when you haven't sweated a lot.

## The role of fibre in physical activity and sport

### Fibre

Fibre is the name given to the indigestible parts of food and it is essential for healthy bowel function. It helps your body absorb vital nutrients as well as remove waste products by providing the bulk that is needed to move them through your digestive system. Fibre also makes you feel fuller for longer so that you eat less and are better able to maintain your optimum weight.

It is important for performers to start their day with a healthy breakfast rich in fibre because it helps the body stay in peak condition.

▲ Fruit, vegetables, brown bread, bran and wholegrain cereals are all high in fibre.

### Activity

7 Keep a food diary for two days, writing down everything you eat and drink, and then use your diary to answer the following questions:
   a) Is your diet balanced? Explain your answer, remembering to think about all seven components of a healthy, balanced diet.
   b) What do you need to add or remove from your diet to make it balanced?

There are many factors that contribute to determining your **optimum weight**, and these factors may change throughout your life.

## Gender

The optimum weight for men tends to be higher than the optimum weight for women. This is because:

- men tend to have a larger skeleton

- men tend to have greater muscle mass.

## Height

Your optimum weight increases the taller you are. This is because taller people have larger skeletons and healthy bones are dense and heavy.

**Factors affecting optimum weight**

## Muscle girth

Muscle girth is the name given to the circumference of a muscle. The bigger your muscle girth the more your muscles weigh, the stronger they are, and the higher your optimum weight. Men tend to have greater muscle girth than women.

## Bone structure

Bigger bones weigh more than smaller bones, so the bigger your skeleton the higher your optimum weight. Your optimum weight also increases the greater your bone density (the solidness of your bones). Bone density is affected by the amount of calcium and vitamin D you consume and you can increase bone density by performing weight bearing exercises. People involved in sports from an early age are likely to have denser bones, which won't break as easily and, as a result, their bones are likely to weigh more.

Because optimum weight is determined by a number of different factors, there is no standard. BMI charts, like the one shown on page 121, are not the most accurate way to measure weight because they can't distinguish between muscle and fat. Sports performers, for example, tend to have a higher optimum weight than non-performers because they have denser bones and bigger muscle girth. It is, therefore, important to consider your percentage of body fat

## Key term

**Optimum weight:** Refers to the weight someone should be, on average, based on their sex, height, bone structure and muscle girth.

when working out your optimum weight. And, if you are concerned about your weight, you should visit a health professional to discuss your concerns.

## How optimum weight varies according to the requirements of different physical activities

◀ These performers are at their optimum weight for their sports. They have a low body weight, low levels of body fat and low muscle girth.

◀ These performers are at their optimum weight for their sports. They have low levels of body fat, but a higher body weight because of their muscle girth. They might be classed as overweight as a result.

◀ These performers are at their optimum weight for their sports. They have high levels of body fat and large muscle girth. They would be classed as obese as a result.

**Energy balance** is the basis of weight control. Once you have reached your optimum weight, you must ensure that the calories you eat are equal to the calories you burn. This is just as true for performers as it is for non-performers, although performers will of course expend more energy and must, therefore, eat more calories.

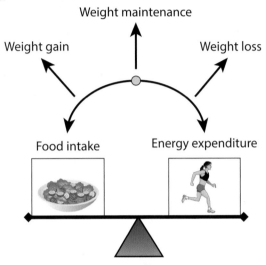

Weight maintenance

Weight gain

Weight loss

Food intake

Energy expenditure

> ### Key term
>
> **Energy balance:** This is the basis of weight control. For body weight to remain constant energy input (via food) must equal energy expenditure.

Performers carrying excess body weight will expend more energy to complete their task, whereas performers who are underweight will not have enough energy to complete their task. Either way, the result is the same. Performers who are not able to maintain a healthy weight are not working as efficiently as they can. They will be slower, weaker and less successful. They are also at greater risk of getting injured and it will take them longer to recover from training sessions and competitions, as well as injuries.

## Activities

9   a)   Search for "Harris Benedict equation" in a search engine and use on online tool to work out how many calories you need to eat each day to maintain a healthy weight. Remember to be honest about how active your lifestyle really is!

    b)   Compare your daily calorie requirements with the daily calorie requirements of your favourite sports performer. Evaluate the extent to which they are the same.

    c)   Compare your favourite sports performer's daily calorie requirements with the daily calories requirements of a partner's favourite sports performer. Discuss why different sports have different daily calorie requirements.

10

How do the dietary requirements of a rugby player and a jockey differ as a result of the different demands placed on their bodies?

# Exam-style questions

**1** Which one of the following is a consequence of living a sedentary lifestyle? (1)
- **A** Weight gain
- **B** Good quality sleep
- **C** Improved fitness levels
- **D** High energy levels

**2** Which one of the following describes the role of fat in a balanced diet? (1)
- **A** It helps gaseous exchange take place
- **B** It provides the body with amino acids
- **C** It is a source of fuel
- **D** It ensures adequate hydration

**3** Which one of the following is **not** an example of a micronutrient? (1)
- **A** Calcium
- **B** Fibre
- **C** Iron
- **D** Sodium

**4** Which one of the following is the correct definition for optimum weight? (1)
- **A** The weight you should be, based on your sex, height, bone structure and muscle girth
- **B** Energy input must equal energy expenditure
- **C** More than your healthy weight
- **D** Body fat that exceeds the healthy amount

**5** Complete the following statements about the exercise young people aged 5 to 18 should do to maintain a basic level of health.

A young person should complete 60 minutes of moderate and vigorous activity per day. ........................................ is an example of an exercise that they can take part in.

It is recommended that young people take part in exercises that help build strong muscles and bones three times per week. An example of a muscle building exercise is ........................................ (2)

**6** Eating a balanced diet is an essential part of a healthy lifestyle.
Explain three ways eating a balanced diet can have a positive impact on our health. (3)

**7** Explain why it is important to maintain hydration during physical activity and sport? (3)

**8** Leading a sedentary lifestyle can have serious consequences.
- **a)** Define the term overweight. (1)
- **b)** State two reasons why weighing more than your optimum weight affects sporting performance. (2)

**9** Evaluate the need for a power athlete to maintain a balanced diet. (9)

**10** Using examples, evaluate how lifestyle choices affect health, fitness and well-being. (9)

# 5 Sport psychology

When you have worked through this chapter, you will have developed knowledge and understanding of:

- the classification of skills
- practice structures
- using goal setting and smart targets to improve and/or optimise performance
- providing guidance and feedback on performance
- mentally preparing for performance.

Skills in physical activity are specific, defined tasks that can be learned and practised. They contribute towards the overall activity.

Each sport or physical activity can be broken down into a group of skills that can be practised. For example, the skills involved in netball include passing, dodging, marking and shooting.

◀ Here we see Joanne Harten performing the skills of shooting and passing in netball.

A number of classifications are used to analyse and describe skills. They group different skills together based on shared characteristics, which is valuable when considering how they should be taught and coached for the most effective outcomes.

The classifications that you need to be aware of are:

- Environmental influence (Closed ⟷ Open)
- Difficulty (Basic ⟷ Complex)
- Organisation level (Low ⟷ High)

Very few skills are, for example, completely closed or completely open. The extremes of each classification are, therefore, placed on a **continuum.**

Extreme A ⟷ Extreme B

**Key terms**

**Skill:** A skill in physical activity is a specific and defined task that can be learned and practised.

**Continuum:** A line with a classification extreme at each end. Skills can then be placed on the continuum; the closer they are placed to the extreme, the more like that extreme they are.

**Exam tip**

Think about "skills" in terms of things that can be learned from start to finish. So don't include things like vision or coordination; think about tackling in hockey, bowling in cricket, or a volley in tennis.

**Exam tip**

Imagine a continuum with "Very tall" at one end and "Very short" at the other end. You would know exactly where to stand if your class was placed on the continuum.

# Environmental influence continuum
## (Closed ⟷ Open)

The environmental influence continuum considers the factors that surround a performer as they execute their skill:

- **Closed skills** are not affected by the environment because they are predictable. The timing of the skill is largely down to the individual involved and there are very few variables that are outside their control.

- **Open skills** are the opposite. They are heavily affected by an unpredictable and changeable environment. The execution of the skill is influenced by conditions of play, teammates and opponents.

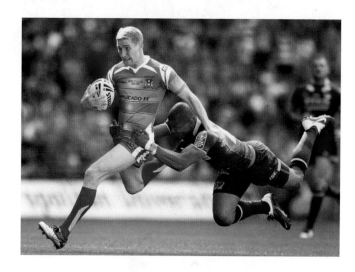

▲ **CLOSED**

Javelin is a very closed skill that should be placed near the "Closed" extreme of the environmental influence continuum. The exact timing of the throw is down to the athlete, who is throwing the same weight javelin in a very similar environment each time.

**OPEN** ▲

A rugby tackle is a very open skill that should be placed near the "Open" extreme of the environmental influence continuum. The timing and style of the tackle is heavily influenced by many factors including the ball carrier, the tackler's teammates and the position on the pitch.

## Key terms

Closed skill: A skill performed in a predictable environment.

Open skill: A skill performed in an unpredictable environment, where the performer has to react and adjust to the changing nature of the situation.

## Exam tip

The exact placement of a skill on a continuum is debateable. It is important to apply the criteria when making a judgement but remember that this is not an exact science so it is good idea to pick obvious examples that are close to the extremes.

## Difficulty continuum (Basic ←→ Complex)

The difficulty continuum considers how complicated skills are and how much attention and concentration is required to complete them:

- **Basic skills** have few sub-routines and require a relatively low level of attention to complete them.

- **Complex skills** are the opposite. They are made up of lots of sub-routines and require great concentration because they are very difficult.

▲ **BASIC**
Running 400 m is a relatively basic skill because it has few sub-routines and a low level of concentration is required to execute it.

**COMPLEX**
The twisting somersault in gymnastics is a complex skill. It has many sub-routines and high levels of concentration are needed to perform it. ▲

# Organisation level continuum (Low ⟷ High)

The organisation continuum considers how tightly knitted together the sub-routines are:

- **Low organisation skills** can be split into sub-routines easily and each sub-routine can be practiced separately.

- **High organisation skills** are seen as whole actions, which must be practised in their entirety.

▲ **LOW**

Swimming (front crawl) has low levels of organisation as it has sub-routines – arm pull, breathing stroke, leg kick and tumble turn – that can be practised separately.

**HIGH**

A golf swing is a highly organised skill because it is almost impossible to break it down into sub-routines when practising it. ▲

## Key terms

**Low organisation skill:** A basic skill that can be broken down easily into different phases so each part can be practised separately.

**High organisation skill:** A skill that cannot be broken down easily and practised separately because the phases of the skill are closely linked.

## Activity

2 Get into small groups. Put two cones down on the floor about 10 metres apart. For each classification, label each cone with one of the extremes from the continuum. Choose a different sporting skill from everyone else in the group and take it in turns to stand on the continuum where you think your skill should be placed. Explain your thinking as you go.

Skills can be developed and improved through effective practice. When selecting the best practice structure to develop a specific skill, it is important to match the skill classification with the most appropriate practice type.

There are four practice structures: fixed practice, variable practice, massed practice and distributed practice.

## Fixed practice

During a **fixed practice** a skill is practised repeatedly in the same way.

This practice structure usually involves drills and, because the environment stays the same and the performer is able to focus solely on the skill itself, it is considered to be an effective way to:

- train someone to perform a closed skill more consistently
- introduce someone to a new skill for the first time.

Examples of closed skills that can be developed effectively using fixed practice include putting in golf, a penalty kick in football, serving in tennis and goal kicking in rugby.

### Exam tip

Always remember to consider the performance level of the learner when deciding on the appropriateness of a practice. What will suit an experienced high-level performer is very different to what a complete beginner will need.

### Key term

**Fixed practice:** Repeatedly practising a whole skill within a training session.

▲ Free throw shooting in basketball is a closed skill and fixed practice is used to make a player's shot as consistent as possible.

## Variable practice

During a **variable practice**, a skill is practised in different settings with unpredictable and changeable conditions.

There is no point practising open skills in a fixed environment. In a game or competition, the environment is likely to change all the time and this needs to be replicated in training. When performing open skills, performers need to be adaptable and variable practice will help them to develop this. The more open the skill and the more experienced the performer, the more variable the practice should be.

### Key term

**Variable practice:** A training session that includes frequent changes of task so that the skill can be repeated in different situations.

▲ A conditioned game is a good example of a variable practice for a team sport. A conditioned game is similar to a full game but certain rules are applied to ensure that players practise a specific skill more often.

### Activity

3  **a)**  Write a list of sporting skills that lend themselves well to fixed practices. Now do the same for variable practices.
   **b)**  Share your lists with a partner. Discuss any differences, justifying your choices.

# Massed practice

**Massed practice** involves long practice periods without rests, where a skill is repeated continuously.

With experienced and motivated performers, this practice structure allows them to increase the consistency of a skill and potentially get used to performing it while they are tired. It lends itself best to practising low organisation or basic skills.

## Key term

**Massed practice:** Practice that occurs without breaks between trials (practice attempts).

▲ Highly motivated and physically fit performers may use massed practice to improve the consistency with which they perform skills that are used repeatedly in their sport.

## Distributed practice

**Distributed practice** has breaks for rest, feedback and mental rehearsal.

Distributed practice has been shown to be the best practice structure for learning new skills because it allows for feedback on performance. It is also seen as better for less-motivated performers who potentially struggle with the repetitive nature of massed practice because the breaks provide an opportunity for rest and praise. Distributed practice is well suited to complex skills that require high concentration.

▲ During distributed practice, a break allows for a rest and feedback on the performance. This is hugely beneficial when learning.

### Use of different practice structures together

Often, fixed practices are massed and variable practices are distributed but this is not always the case.

Good coaches will have an understanding of which practices suit the skills being developed and the performers developing them. Both will influence which practice structure will get the best results. Also, depending on the different objectives of a training session, more than one practice structure may be used.

**Goal setting** is very important in sport and exercise as it links closely with motivation. Effective goal setting allows performers to improve and optimise their performance by giving training purpose and focus. Goals increase the chances of a person making improvements and being increasingly successful over time.

Effective goal setting can:

- allow analysis of current strengths and weaknesses
- give a performer something attainable to aim for
- improve focus
- increase effort
- develop perseverance
- supply additional motivation
- improve overall performance.

### Key term

**Goal setting:** The process of setting down targets that a performer will aim to accomplish.

### Exam tip

Think of your target grades at school. Why do you have them? How do they make you think and feel when you get results back? Would you think and feel differently without them? If you think about why you have target grades in school and what they do, you'll be able to give a great answer to the question, "Why is goal setting important in sport and exercise?"

### Activity

5   On the start line of any marathon, there will be lots of people with completely different goals to each other. Provided that the goals are appropriate for each individual, there is a chance that many will finish the race feeling successful even though just one person was able to win the race.

   **a)** Discuss how lots of participants in a marathon can finish the race with a sense of success, even though they did not win the race.

   **b)** Describe three different goals that a marathon runner might have.

The way that goals are set is crucial. Setting goals that are too general and bordering on unattainable will only serve to demotivate performers; the exact opposite of what is wanted. Effective goals should be set by applying the principles of **SMART targets**.

### Key term

**SMART targets:** An acronym used to guide the setting of effective goals. SMART targets are **S**pecific, **M**easurable, **A**chievable, **R**ealistic and **T**ime-bound.

### Exam tip

Collecting quantitative data on a regular basis can help you measure whether or not you are on track to achieve your goals.

### Achievable

Goals should be within the reach of the performer. They should be challenging but attainable. This is valuable because a performer will become demotivated if they don't achieve a goal. They are also unlikely to chase a goal they do not think is achievable.

### Measurable

You must have a way of knowing if you have achieved your goals. Goals should, therefore, contain a time or something similar. This is valuable because it allows a definite 'met' or 'not met' statement to be made.

### Realistic

It should be possible for the performer to actually hit the goals set, if they work hard and progress well. The value in this is making the performer aspire to reach a goal that they feel is possible.

### Specific

Goals should target a specific aspect of performance to develop, which it is possible to actively focus on. This is valuable because it ensures the goal emphasises a definite training need.

### Time-bound

Goals should have time limits. If they don't, a performer will always be working towards a goal, with no real rush to get there and no given point when they will be able to decide if they have been successful. This is valuable because a performer can assess whether or not they have hit their goal at a given point, or not.

**M A R S T**

Here are some examples of SMART targets:

- 100 m sprinter: Take 0.2 sec off my personal best time by the last race of the season.

- Striker in football: Score 12 goals this season compared to 9 last season.

- Rugby goal kicker: To improve my season's kicking percentage by 5% compared to last season.

- Trampolinist: To raise my tariff by 0.5 by the end of next month.

- Marathon runner: To take 2 minutes off my personal best in the marathon at the end of the month.

## Reviewing targets

It is not enough to set goals and work towards them. You must review the targets set and decide whether or not success has been achieved:

- If the goals have been met, then new targets should be set to ensure continued motivation and to push the individual on to improve further.

- If the goals have not been met, then the process of evaluating why this was the case can often be extremely beneficial and inform future training, and future goal setting.

### Activity

6   Consider an area of your life where you would like to see some improvement. What is your goal? It could relate to sport and exercise or your life more generally. Write down SMART targets to help you achieve your goal. Make sure your SMART targets meet all five criteria.

▲ If a measurable goal has been set, like winning the Rugby World Cup 2014, it is easy to know if it has been achieved. However, in most cases, it is necessary to review targets carefully to determine whether or not goals have been met.

# Types of guidance to optimise performance

**Key term**

**Guidance:** Information to aid the learning of a skill.

**Guidance** is the information given to someone to help them develop a skill, to improve and optimise their performance. There are four types of guidance:

▲ Visual guidance

▲ Verbal guidance

▲ Manual guidance

▲ Mechanical guidance

The type of guidance used will depend on the skills being developed and the performers who are involved in the session.

## Visual guidance

**Visual guidance** is when guidance is presented in a form that the performer can look at. It can include anything from a live demonstration to a video or a film, a poster, a chart or court markings.

**Key term**

**Visual guidance:** Information given to a performer to help them develop that they can see.

▲ Visual guidance: A coach or higher-level performer demonstrates basketball shooting skills to a group of young players.

When using visual guidance, it is important that the technique being shown is of good quality. It is also important that those learning watch closely and pay attention to the key points.

**Advantages**

✓ Useful for all levels of performer.

✓ Especially good for young/inexperienced performers.

✓ Vision is most people's dominant sense.

✓ Allows performers to see what is required.

✓ Specific aspects of a whole skill can be observed.

✓ Performers can copy what they have seen.

**Disadvantages**

✗ Demonstration or image must be of good quality.

✗ Some skills are too complex to demonstrate.

✗ Not effective if performers are not paying attention.

# Verbal guidance

**Verbal guidance** is when a coach describes how to perform a skill or tells a performer something.

▲ Verbal guidance: Coaches talk to performers and explain what is being done well and how they can improve.

## Key term

**Verbal guidance:** Information given to a performer to help them develop that they can hear. It involves someone telling them something.

## Exam tip

Different types of guidance will often be used in combination with each other. For example, a demonstration where key features are highlighted and discussed is a good combination of visual and verbal guidance.

## Activity

**7** Think about the last PE lesson you had or the last training session you were involved in. What types of guidance did your teacher or coach use? Do you think these were the most appropriate for that session? Why?

## Advantages

✓ Especially useful for higher-level performers.

✓ Good way of highlighting key teaching points.

✓ Useful for sharing basic information and instructions.

✓ Questioning can often make a performer think.

## Disadvantages

✗ Can result in "information overload".

✗ Can be boring.

✗ Sports arenas are often noisy.

✗ Complex things are often difficult to explain.

# Manual guidance

**Manual guidance** involves a coach physically moving a performer into the correct position or supporting them as they perform a skill.

▲ Manual guidance: A coach will move a performer into the correct position so they can feel how the skill is meant to feel when done correctly.

## Advantages

✓ Good for complete beginners.

✓ Allows some development of correct feel.

## Disadvantages

✗ A movement can feel different when someone else is moving your body for you.

✗ Performer may not think that they're actually performing it themselves.

# Mechanical guidance

**Mechanical guidance** takes place when equipment is used to assist in the coaching process. This could take the form of floats in swimming or harnesses in diving, gymnastics and trampolining.

## Key term

**Mechanical guidance:** Information given to a performer to help them develop that involves equipment to assist in the learning process.

## Activity

8 Discuss which types of guidance you might use if you were teaching/coaching the following and how your chosen type of guidance would benefit the performer.
   a) A beginner in badminton.
   b) A beginner in gymnastics.
   c) A local club level footballer.
   d) A local club level netballer.
   e) An advanced triple jumper.
   f) An advanced golfer.

◀ Mechanical guidance: Equipment is used to allow complex skills to be performed safely or to build confidence.

## Advantages

✓ Good for potentially dangerous skills.

✓ Can allow performer to gain a feel for a movement without fear.

✓ Good for building confidence.

## Disadvantages

✗ Equipment may be expensive.

✗ Performer can come to rely on the aid.

# 5.6 Types of feedback to optimise performance

**Exam tip**

It is easy to fall into the trap of thinking that feedback comes from a coach. This is only one way of receiving feedback. You'll need to be very open about how you think about the term feedback.

**Feedback** is information that a performer has access to during or after a performance. This information can take many forms but all feedback will give the performer some idea about how successful they have been.

There are four types of feedback: **intrinsic feedback** and **extrinsic feedback**, **concurrent feedback** and **terminal feedback**.

## Key terms

**Feedback:** Information received during or after a performance about the performance.

**Intrinsic feedback:** Information a performer receives about their performance that comes from within and is linked to how a movement feels.

**Extrinsic feedback:** Information a performer receives about their performance from a coach.

**Concurrent feedback:** Information a performer receives about their performance during the activity.

**Terminal feedback:** Information a performer receives about their performance after the activity has been completed.

## Intrinsic feedback

Intrinsic feedback comes from within. It relates to how a movement feels, which is known as kinesthetic feel. Inexperienced performers will not be able to rely on this feedback because they will not have a developed knowledge and understanding of how skills should feel. In contrast, experienced performers have developed knowledge and understanding of kinesthetic feel and will know if a movement is correct or incorrect. They will be much more capable of self-assessing and self-correcting because of their extra experience.

Feedback is either intrinsic or extrinsic. ↔

## Extrinsic feedback

Extrinsic feedback comes from a coach. The feedback will normally come in the form of visual or verbal guidance as a coach relays what the performer did right and wrong, and shows or tells them how they looked. Less-experienced performers need this kind of feedback to let them know how they have done and motivate and encourage them to keep trying. More-experienced performers are likely to use extrinsic feedback with intrinsic feedback to gain a full picture of how they did before deciding on what needs to be improved.

## Concurrent feedback

Concurrent feedback takes place during the performance and can be intrinsic or extrinsic. If an activity lasts long enough, a performer can make adjustments as they go. They could feel that they're doing something wrong and alter it or a coach could verbally instruct them to make a change.

Feedback is either concurrent or terminal. ↔

## Terminal feedback

Terminal feedback is received after the performance. It could come straight away or some time later, but it always comes from an extrinsic feedback source. A coach could talk the performer through what they saw or the performer could watch a replay. Many sports teams run full video analysis sessions with their players, which are an example of terminal feedback.

## Activity

9

A

B

C

D

**a)** Discuss the photos and decide, for each photo, which types of feedback would be possible. Think about the length of each activity and whether a coach could give feedback during the activity or would have to wait until after it has finished.

**b)** During your next practical lesson, gather lots of different types of feedback on your performance and consider the benefits of each type in relation to the others. Think about how the type of activity impacts on the type of feedback that it is possible to receive.

With technology now heavily involved in sport, lots of performance-related data is collected. Many sports, including cricket, basketball and American football, collect a lot of data that can be used to give the performer detailed feedback on their performance. It is usually presented graphically to make it easier to interpret and analyse.

Performance-related data is usually delivered as extrinsic and terminal feedback, but coaches can now receive data during a game making it concurrent feedback. This data can affect the messages that are passed to performers and can also influence substitutions and tactical changes.

### Exam tip DATA

A trend is a direction of movement. It describes the general direction in which something is developing at any given moment. Analysing trends in quantitative data allows you make predictions about what will happen in the future.

## Activities DATA

**10** These are pitch maps produced by Hawkeye to show where bowlers, in cricket, have pitched their deliveries.

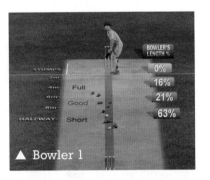

▲ Bowler 1

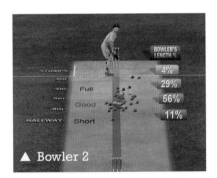

▲ Bowler 2

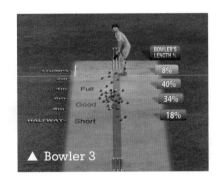

▲ Bowler 3

**a)** Interpret the data: Which bowler bowled the highest percentage of short balls?

**b)** Present the data as three pie charts.

**c)** Analyse the data: How would this kind of feedback on performance be useful to a bowler?

**11** The graph shows how the personal best of a young triple jumper developed during an athletics season.

**a)** Interpret the graph: Is the current trend upwards or downwards? Explain your answer.

**b)** Present the data by producing a line graph showing the same information as this bar graph.

**c)** Analyse the data: Make a prediction based on your analysis. What would you expect August's data to show?

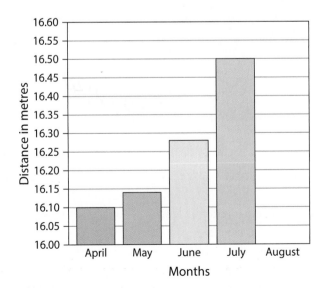

▲ A bar graph showing the personal bests of a young triple jumper, by month.

Effective mental preparation ahead of sports performance has shown to be highly effective. Sport psychologists are now employed by most professional sports teams to ensure that performers are in the best place psychologically to succeed.

## Psychological warm-up

Good mental preparation during a warm-up – a **psychological warm-up** – ensures that all of a performer's attention is totally focused on the performance and nothing is able to distract from the task at hand. It helps a performer manage their nerves and control outside pressures.

Each performer will have their own preferred methods of preparing during their warm-up. Some may use positive self-talk, where they talk to themselves using positive phrases, to keep them confident and push away doubts. Some may use trigger words to remind them of important teaching points that they must remember. Some may recap some of their most relevant goals.

Periods of stretching may also allow a performer to carry out breathing exercises and relaxation techniques.

> **Key term**
>
> **Psychological warm-up:** A performer gets mentally ready to give their very best.

▼ Many sports performers, like Laura Trott, will listen to music during parts of a warm-up. This may help them relax or they may have a playlist of songs that motivate them for what's ahead.

Many sports now follow the example set in rugby and hold a final huddle before kick-off. This allows for some last minute motivational words and a chance for final focus to be added.

## Mental rehearsal

**Mental rehearsal** is a technique that many high-level performers use before they perform skills that have specific preparation time. During mental rehearsal you practise the skill in your head; you act out the movements in your head to remind yourself how it feels to perform them successfully.

▲ Diving, rugby goal kicking and golf are all examples of skills that allow for mental rehearsal. This allows performers to block out distractions, increase their focus and make their execution consistent.

**Activity**

**12** Carry out a mental rehearsal experiment:

- Make sure everyone in the class has a tennis ball or a piece of screwed up paper.

- Stand or sit in a circle around a central bin or bucket and take it in turns to practise throwing the ball into the bin a few times, so that you get a feel for it.

- Split the class in half, ensuring that both halves have a mixture of people who are good at the task and people who are weaker at the task. Half will be the "go" group and half will be the "mentally rehearse and go when you're ready" group.

- On an instruction, each member of the "go" group will quickly, without time to think, throw their ball into the bin one after the other. How many go in?

- Next, on a second instruction, the "mentally rehearse and go when you're ready" group will take it in turns to do just that. Each person should look at the target, imagine the action of throwing, gain a feel in their muscles for how the action is carried out successfully, take a deep breath and then throw. How many go in?

# Exam-style questions

1   Which one of the following is the best example of a closed skill? (1)
    **A**   A volley in tennis
    **B**   Passing to a teammate in hockey
    **C**   Putting in golf
    **D**   An attacking header in football

2   Which one of the following is a benefit for goal setting in sport? (1)
    **A**   Makes you beat your personal best each time
    **B**   Increases motivation
    **C**   Means you don't need to train as often
    **D**   Decreases the effort you need

3   Which one of the following is a reason for distributed practice suiting beginners? (1)
    **A**   Allows breaks for rest and feedback
    **B**   It means they can improve their fitness
    **C**   Makes them more motivated
    **D**   Stops them only learning closed skills

4   Which one of the following practice types would be recommended for very open skills? (1)
    **A**   Open practice
    **B**   Optional practice
    **C**   Massed practice
    **D**   Variable practice

5   Goal setting in sport is said to improve or optimise performance.
    Describe the benefits of goal setting. (3)

6   Skills can be classified on a continuum from basic to complex.
    Using an example, describe what makes a skill:
    **a)**   Basic (2)
    **b)**   Complex (2)

7   Assess how beneficial manual and mechanical guidance can be when learning a new skill. (4)

▲ **Figure 1**

8   **Figure 1** shows a rugby player preparing to take a kick at goal.
    **a)**   Describe the mental rehearsal process. (2)
    **b)**   Explain the possible benefits of mental rehearsal for the rugby player. (2)

9   Evaluate the relative importance of intrinsic and extrinsic feedback for an experienced badminton player and someone just beginning to learn the game. (9)

10  Evaluate the importance of SMART targets in the goal setting of a long distance runner. (9)

# 6 Socio-cultural influences

When you have worked through this chapter, you will have developed knowledge and understanding of:

- engagement patterns of different social groups in physical activity and sport

- commercialisation of physical activity and sport

- ethical and socio-cultural issues in physical activity and sport.

Taking part in sport and physical activity has hugely positive impacts on a person's well-being. As a result, monitoring participation rates is essential to ensuring that everything possible is done to promote sport and physical activity, and provide as many people as possible with opportunities to get involved.

One major benefit of monitoring participation rates is that target groups can be identified. Target groups are groups of people that are under-represented in sport and physical activity because they have specific barriers to participation. Once identified, plans can be developed to make it easier for each target group to access opportunities to take part.

Availability of provision is a significant barrier for many target groups. For example, fewer people will be attracted to play wheelchair football than will be attracted to play able-bodied five-a-side football, so a leisure centre that is run for profit is more likely to include five-a-side football in their timetable than wheelchair football. This makes it difficult for people with a disability, who want to play wheelchair football, to find somewhere to participate.

Many barriers to participation are caused by stereotyping and prejudice in society, stopping individuals who otherwise may participate actively in sport and physical activity.

Participation rates in physical activity and sport can be affected by a number of personal factors. These include:

- gender
- age
- socio-economic group
- ethnicity
- disability.

## Gender

**Snapshot from Sport England**

 **SPORT ENGLAND**

2015 data shows:

"Currently 40.6% of men play sport at least once a week, compared to 30.7% of women. At a younger age, men are much more likely than women to play sport. But this difference declines sharply with age."

Gender affects participation, with more boys and men involved in physical activity and sport than girls and women.

While in certain activity areas physical differences between men and women can influence participation, social stereotyping is the major reason why fewer girls and women get involved in physical activity and sport.

**Exam tip**

It is important to understand the benefits of sport and physical activity alongside the barriers that can prevent certain people participating. The positive impacts of participation are discussed on pages 110–12.

**Activity**

1  a)  Identify possible target groups that are under-represented in sport and physical activity.

   b)  Discuss how stereotypes may lead to an under-representation of these target groups in specific sports.

**Exam tip**

Use the mnemonic "Great Athletes Survive Every Distance" to remember the five personal factors that influence participation rates.

In the past, women's opportunities were often limited in many areas of life, including sport. For example, until 1972, women were not permitted to compete in Olympic events longer than 800 m because the distances were seen as too strenuous for them. Today, women compete in all events, with great success, proving how ill-informed this thinking was.

Although society's attitude towards women is now different, stereotyping still exists. As a result, women sometimes feel they need to participate in physical activities that are less competitive, such as yoga and aerobics, rather than get involved in a full range of sporting activities like rugby and basketball. Women, sometimes more than men, also juggle many different things in their lives, including working, looking after children and elderly parents and looking after a home. This can make it difficult for them to find time to take part in physical activity and sport.

Public support for the successful women's rugby, football and netball world cup teams has given female sport in the United Kingdom a superb boost to increase female participation rates. Change will come as a result of the media working harder to publicise women's sports. This will increase the number of well-known female sporting role models, in turn giving more girls and women the confidence to take part in sport and exercise.

Opportunities for girls and women to participate locally also need to increase. Eventually, it is hoped that women's teams will be as well-funded as male teams at local as well as regional and national level.

### Activity

2   Go through the list of activities linked to your GCSE PE course and divide them into two groups:
   ● Activities where men and women compete separately.
   ● Activities where men and women compete together.
   Why do you think this division occurs?

▼ Brilliant coaches like Becky Hammon, who was the first female assistant coach of a male NBA team, are crucial to the development of women's sport. She has shown the world that gender doesn't need to be a barrier to participation and success, even in traditionally male-dominated environments.

▲ Sport England's "This girl can" campaign is an example of the work being done to increase the participation of a target group. It is designed to get more girls and women involved in sport and physical activity by celebrating participation.

## Age

**Snapshot from Sport England**

2015 data shows:

"54.8% of 16-to-25-year-olds take part in at least one sport session a week, compared to 31.9% of older adults (26 plus)."

Participation in sport and physical activity tends to peak between 16 and 25, when people have most free time. Engaging young people is crucial, because those who are actively involved in physical activity and sport at an early age are more likely to participate throughout their lives. This is the major reason why school and youth sport receives a lot of funding.

◀ Early involvement in sport is key to lifelong participation.

Throughout their working lives many people have very little free time and disposable income (the money you have left over to spend on recreation after you have paid for the basics, including food, shelter, energy and clothing) to spend on physical activity and sport, as they focus on their careers and their families. The physical changes caused by ageing also have a huge impact on participation.

Flexibility decreases with age.

Your overall level of general fitness decreases as you get older.

**Ageing can affect participation**

▲ Staying active throughout your life can improve your quality of life.

Having reached full strength at around the age of 25, strength begins to decrease from around the age of 40.

The older you are the more likely you are to suffer from ill-health, which will affect your ability to participate.

Tidal volume and stroke volume decrease with age and vascular shunting becomes less efficient.

Older people are more likely to suffer injuries, and will take longer to recover from those injuries.

Although the body changes as you age, and this might have an impact on the level at which you compete or the frequency and intensity with which you train, people of all ages can, and should, exercise regularly to improve their well-being. Many people, therefore, change the type of physical activity they are involved in, as they get older.

**Activity**

**3** Research the range of sports and physical activities that are on offer at your local leisure centre. Does the centre cater for all age groups? Are there any age groups that are under-represented or over-represented? Can you suggest reasons why?

▲ "Life sports" like lawn bowls, golf and swimming provide people of all ages with an opportunity to continue to participate in physical activity and sport because they don't place as much stress on your body as other sports.

## Socio-economic group

**Snapshot from Sport England**

 **SPORT ENGLAND**

2015 data shows:

Participation "is highest among managerial/professional workers and intermediate social groups. It is lowest among manual workers and unemployed people."

Taking part in physical activity and sport comes with a financial cost. Whether it is buying equipment, paying membership fees or travelling to and from training, sport can be expensive. This means that the amount of disposable income a person has affects their participation.

People at the top of the socio-economic scale, who have highly paid jobs and a lot of disposable income, are more likely to participate in physical activity and sport. People lower down the socio-economic scale, who work in low-paid jobs, are unemployed or can't work, and so have very little disposable income, are less likely to participate. The richer areas of the country may also have better facilities than the poorer areas of the country, which also impacts on participation.

Participation among people lower on the socio-economic scale in expensive sports such as skiing, sailing, rowing and horse riding, is very low. In contrast, sports like football and basketball are often popular because it does not cost a lot of money to participate.

◀ Wayne Rooney became a professional footballer at a very early age. His family did not have a lot of disposable income when he was growing up, but professional sport has given him the opportunity to become very wealthy.

It is important to remember that your socio-economic background does not have to be a barrier to participation. If you want to try canoeing, for example, then ask around and see if you can join a subsidised trip to a canoe centre, or talk to your teachers about the possibility of local sporting grants.

## Ethnicity

### Snapshot from Sport England

2015 data shows:

"The number of both black and minority ethnic and white British adults playing sport is increasing."

The term "ethnicity" describes the ethnic group you belong to. An ethnic group is a social group that shares cultural traditions, a religion or other factors.

As a multicultural society, it could be assumed that participation in physical activity and sport in the UK would be the same across all ethnic groups but this is not always the case.

Data shows that participation by people from an ethnic minority background is often limited to sports and physical activities that are stereotypically associated with that ethnic group. Also, while it appears that ethnic minority groups are well represented in professional sport, this doesn't always translate to participation among the general population. The numbers of professional captains, managers and coaches from ethnic minority backgrounds also remains at a relatively low level.

▲ It is important that performers from ethnic minority backgrounds, who have risen to the top of their sports, become role models to help increase participation among ethnic minority groups.

**Activity**

4   Find out about "Sporting Equals" or the Football Association's "Kick it Out" campaign. Why was the organisation or campaign set up? What does it want to achieve and how?

◀ Prejudice against people from ethnic minority groups often results in people shying away from participating. Initiatives that tackle prejudice, like "Sporting Equals" and the Football Association's "Kick it Out" campaign, are fighting for equal opportunities for all and educating the public about acceptable behaviour.

# Disability

**Snapshot from Sport England**

 **SPORT ENGLAND**

2015 data shows:

"17.2% of disabled people are playing sport regularly, up from 15.1% in 2005/6."

Disability is defined by the government as a physical or mental impairment that has a substantial and long-term negative effect on a person's ability to carry out normal daily activities. It can, therefore, significantly affect a person's participation in sport and physical activity. However, national governing bodies make efforts to ensure their sports are accessible to all and participation rates of people with disabilities are on the increase.

Nevertheless, there are significant barriers that continue to affect the ability of people with disabilities to take part in sport and physical activity. There are a limited number of teachers and coaches with the necessary qualifications, and not all local facilities have been fully adapted to cater for people with disabilities. People with disabilities can also find travelling problematic and may be reliant on disability benefits, which limits their disposable income.

The increased media coverage and popularity of the London 2012 Paralympics is a sign that achievements of sportspeople with disabilities are beginning to be recognised and celebrated publically. Such support and media coverage is likely to inspire more disabled people to get involved in sport and physical activity over time.

**Activity**

5 Boccia, polybat, wheelchair football and goalball are specialist sports that can be played by people with disabilities. Prepare a short presentation on the rules and regulations of a specialist sport of your choice.

◄ Ellie Simmonds, a swimmer, decided she was going to the Paralympics in 2004, when she was nine years old. By the end of the London 2012 Paralympics she had won seven Olympic gold medals.

## Activities

DATA

**6** Study these two graphs:

**a)** Interpret **Figure 1**: What does the graph tell you about the number of countries sending competitors to the Paralympic Games between 1960 and 2012?

**b)** Interpret **Figure 2**: What does the graph tell you about the number of competitors taking part in the Paralympic Games between 1960 and 2012?

**c)** Analyse the data: Make a prediction based on your analysis of the trends illustrated by the graphs. What would you expect 2016's data to show?

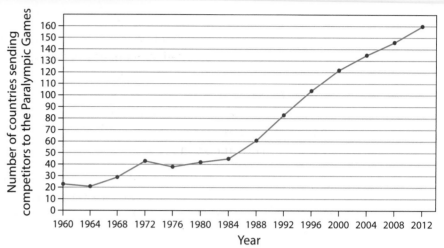

▲ **Figure 1**

*Source: www.paralympic.org*

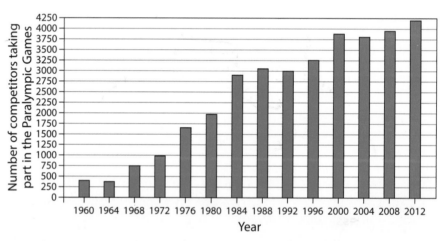

▲ **Figure 2**

*Source: www.paralympic.org*

**7** Write some questions for your partner to answer about this graph:

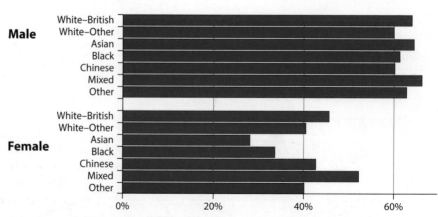

▲ **Figure 3**: This graph shows participation by ethnic group for 16–25-year-olds.

*Source: Sport England*

# The commercialisation of physical activity and sport

**Commercialisation** is the act of making something available for purchase, with the aim of making profit. The commercialisation of physical activity and sport involves individuals, organisations and companies buying and selling sporting goods and services with a focus on profit rather than participation. The more people want to watch and take part in certain sports, and the more money they are willing to pay to do this, the greater the opportunity to make money and the more commercialised the sport becomes.

The media has played a central role in commercialising physical activity and sport because the more exposure that it gives to sport, the greater the potential for businesses to earn money from it. For example, a company that sponsors a team playing in the English Premier League will have its name and logo broadcast all over the world and will be associated with the success of the team.

> ## Key term
>
> **Commercialisation:** The commercialisation of physical activity and sport involves individuals, organisations and companies buying and selling sporting goods and services with a focus on profit rather than participation.

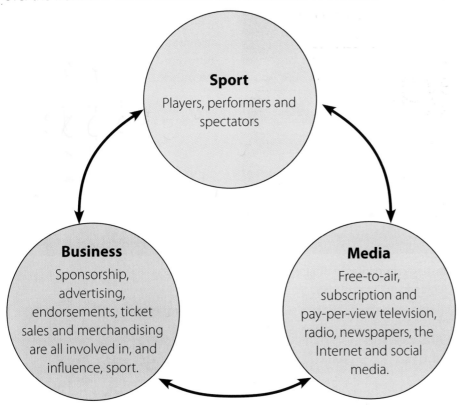

## How has media coverage contributed to the commercialisation of sport and physical activity?

Television companies pay to broadcast elite matches and competitions, and this money is used to pay the wages of players and performers. For example, Manchester City pay their players an average of £96,445 per week.

The media can influence how sport is organised to suit its own business interests. For example, British Sky Broadcasting encouraged the Premier League to break away from the Football League in 1992.

Many sports have been adapted so that they are better to watch for the television audience. For example, kick off times for Premiership football matches are regularly moved so that broadcasters can maximise their audiences and, as a result, the money they get from selling advertising during ad breaks. Similarly, the seven-point tiebreak was introduced in tennis to speed things up when a game is tied at 6–6 because the unpredictable length of games was causing problems for television schedules.

The number of teams taking part in the FIFA World Cup was increased from 16 in 1934, to 24 in 1982, and to 32 in 1998 to ensure maximum viewing figures around the world. This is because the more people who watch the World Cup the more FIFA can charge broadcasters for the rights to televise matches.

◀ One Day Internationals and Twenty20 cricket matches are played in coloured kit, rather than traditional cricket whites, to make the game more appealing to spectators and sponsors. It also means that revenue can be generated by selling shirts to the public.

## Activity

8 This table shows the fees paid by broadcasting companies in different parts of the world to broadcast the Olympic Games, in millions of US$.

| | North America (USA and Canada) | Central America, South America and the Caribbean | Asia | Middle East and Africa | Europe | Oceania | Total |
|---|---|---|---|---|---|---|---|
| 1998–2000 | 1124 | 14 | 208 | 12 | 422 | 65 | 1845 |
| 2002–2004 | 1397 | 21 | 233 | 13 | 514 | 54 | 2232 |
| 2006–2008 | 1579 | 34 | 274 | 25 | 578 | 80 | 2570 |
| 2010–2012 | 2154 | 106 | 575 | 41 | 848 | 126 | 3850 |

*Source: www.olympic.org*

**a)** Interpret the data: Which part of the world has paid most to broadcast the Olympic Games in their territory?

**b)** Analyse the data: What impact do you think this has on the way the Olympic Games is organised?

# The advantages and disadvantages of commercialisation and the media

Commercialisation and the huge influence of the media have both advantages and disadvantages for individual sports, for players and performers, for spectators and for sponsors.

## Key term

**Grassroots participation:** This is participation in sport and physical activity that takes place at the local level. It often involves lots of volunteers who organise and coach training sessions and competitions for the love of the sport.

|  | Advantages | Disadvantages |
|---|---|---|
| **Sport**<br> | • more sports are attracting media attention, increasing **grassroots participation**<br>• more money is available for teams, equipment, facilities, coaches and players<br>• prize funds and rewards for winning are bigger<br>• more money is spent on technological developments that can help performance<br>• there are more competitions, increasing the reach of the sport<br>• more role models and ambassadors for the sport are created | • rules are changed to meet the requirements of the media and sponsors<br>• over-exposure can cause people to lose interest in a sport as both grassroots participants and supporters<br>• minor sports and women's sport get less coverage<br>• controversies become sensationalised<br>• sports depend on money from the media and sponsors, with disastrous results if it is withdrawn<br>• sponsors may sell products or services that promote poor lifestyle choices |
| **Player/performer** | • players are paid higher wages<br>• the media can turn players/performers into heroes and role models<br>• more money to pay for technologically advanced equipment and facilities<br>• more money to pay for better coaching and training programmes<br>• more competitions raises the standard of competition nationally and increases a national team's profile internationally<br>• more money to support grassroots players/performers, which benefits those who take part in the sport for fun and provides progression for those wanting to compete at the highest level | • a strong media presence can increase the pressure to perform and can reduce the players'/performers' enjoyment<br>• the media spotlight can mean that the mistakes a player/performer makes become very public<br>• sponsors may dictate a player's/performer's behaviour, which can disrupt training<br>• maintaining appeal to sponsors and media can distract players/performers from training<br>• intense media scrutiny of players'/performers' private lives, particularly for women<br>• more competitions means more training, and overtraining can lead to injury<br>• too many competitions can reduce the standard of competition<br>• women players/performers are paid less than men, largely because media and sponsors focus on men<br>• the achievements of one or two players can be emphasised at the expense of the team |

> ## Exam tip
>
> When discussing the advantages and disadvantages of commercialisation and the media, it is important to use specific examples to illustrate each advantage and each disadvantage.

| | Advantages | Disadvantages |
|---|---|---|
| **Spectator**<br> | • events are scheduled so supporters can easily watch them on TV or online<br>• commentary, which is not available to a spectator watching live, educates the viewer at home<br>• live coverage, highlights, documentaries and coaching tips satisfy the spectator's interest in the sports they follow and educate them<br>• the media provides information about results, fixtures and rankings<br>• money has been spent on technology to improve viewing, including instant replay and close-up views of the action<br>• more competitions give more spectators the opportunity to watch their sport live<br>• more media coverage of player's/performers' activities outside of sport makes spectators feel better connected to their role models | • more people stay at home to watch<br>• most sport is now shown via subscription and pay-per-view services, making it expensive to watch<br>• tickets and merchandise are expensive<br>• demands made by sponsors can limit choice and value-for-money for spectators when they are buying food and drink etc. at live events<br>• the more popular a sport becomes, the more difficult it is to buy tickets<br>• scheduling for home-viewing makes it more difficult for people who want to watch sport live |
| **Sponsor**<br> | • a sponsor's name or brand is linked to a positive, healthy, triumphant activity and advertised to a wide audience, increasing the profits for the brand owner | • if a sponsor links their name or brand to a sport, team or player/performer that is hit by a scandal, it can have a damaging effect on its reputation and, therefore, its profits |

## Activity

**9** Here is some data about the number of people over 16, in millions, participating in cycling once a month:

| 2006–07 | 2007–08 | 2008–09 | 2009–10 | 2010–11 | 2011–12 | 2012–13 | 2013–14 | 2014–15 |
|---|---|---|---|---|---|---|---|---|
| 3.55 | 3.9 | 4.2 | 4.01 | 3.9 | 3.8 | 3.79 | 3.88 | 3.81 |

*Source: www.sportengland.org*

**a)** Plot the data on a graph.

**b)** Interpret the data: What does the data tell you about participation rates for cycling over the nine years?

**c)** Analyse the data: make a prediction based on your analysis. What would you expect the data for 2015–16 to show?

# Different types of sporting behaviour

There are two different types of sporting behaviour, **gamesmanship** and **sportsmanship**.

Gamesmanship encourages performers to focus on success and to bend the rules of their sport as much as they can without actually breaking them in order to succeed. Sportsmanship brings the qualities of fair play, following the rules and being gracious in defeat or victory. This provides checks and balances to ensure that gamesmanship does not become **deviant behaviour**. Deviant behaviour is behaviour that goes against the moral values or rules of a sport.

## Key terms

**Gamesmanship:** Bending the rules/laws of a sport without actually breaking them.

**Sportsmanship:** The qualities of fairness, following the rules and being gracious in defeat or victory.

**Deviant behaviour:** Behaviour that goes against the moral values or rules of a sport.

◄ Sportsmanship in action: The England cricket team gave Australian captain Michael Clarke a guard of honour when he came out to bat in his final test match in 2015.

◄ You can see gamesmanship in action when, in basketball, teams deliberately foul bad free throw shooters. For example, teams target DeAndre Jordan of the Los Angeles Clippers to make him shoot a free throw, knowing he has a very poor record and they will gain possession as a result.

# The reasons for, and consequences of, deviant behaviour at elite level

When a player, performer, coach or even a spectator displays deviant behaviour it has a negative effect on the individual involved, on the sporting community and on our wider society. It is, therefore, important for players and performers at all levels to demonstrate sportsmanship and model the values of fair play. This is particularly important for players at an elite level as they often have strong media profiles and are seen by many as role models. Their behaviour, whether good or bad, is likely to be copied by others, especially young people who idolise sports stars.

Here are some examples of deviant behaviour.

## Activity

**10** Diving in football: gamesmanship or deviant behaviour? Some people argue that if a player feels contact, then he is entitled to fall. They claim that this is simply gamesmanship, and that defenders shouldn't make rash challenges. Other people feel that this is outright cheating or deviant behaviour and should be stamped out of the game. What do you think?

▲ Using performance enhancing drugs, like Lance Armstrong.

▲ Diego Maradona's hand ball against England during the 1986 World Cup, known as "The hand of God".

◄ Taking bribes to influence the outcome of a match or competition, like Salman Butt, Mohammad Asif and Mohammad Amir, three top Pakistani cricketers who took bribes to bowl deliberate no-balls.

▲ Violence, on or off the field of play, like Luis Suarez who bit Italy defender Giorgio Chiellini during the 2014 Fifa World Cup.

The consequences of deviant behaviour at elite level are serious. They include:

- on the field: penalties being awarded and being booked or being sent off, which can result in your team losing a match or a competition
- off the field: receiving fines, bans and point deductions for yourself and for your team
- losing your contract with your team, club or sponsor
- receiving or inflicting a career-ending injury
- damaging your own reputation, among your peers and more widely
- damaging the reputation of your club, team, country and sport.

So, if the consequences are so serious, why do elite performers break the rules? Every performer who displays deviant behaviour will have their own particular set of reasons for acting as they did, but there are some reasons that come up time and again.

Many say that the pressure to win is overwhelming and they feel forced – by themselves, by their teammates, by their coaches, by the media and by supporters – to win at all costs. Winning also brings fame and fortune and the lure of riches can make people do things they know are wrong. And many simply lose their tempers and lash out without thinking when an official makes a decision they think is unfair, or when someone they are competing against does something they don't like.

### Exam tip

When discussing sportsmanship, gamesmanship and deviant behaviour, it is important to use specific examples to illustrate each point you make.

### Activity DATA

11 Choose one elite performer that has displayed deviant behaviour and produce a short podcast documentary about what they did, why they did it and what the consequences of their actions were.

### Activity

12 Go to the UK Anti-Doping's website and follow the links to find the list of performers currently serving bans for violating anti-doping rules. Answer these questions:
   a) Interpret the data: Which sport has the most bans?
   b) Analyse the data: Why do you think this is?

# Exam-style questions

1. Which one of the following is **not** an advantage of commercialisation in sport? (1)
   - **A** Increases interest in sport
   - **B** Over exposure of sport
   - **C** More money available for equipment/resources
   - **D** More role models

2. **Figure 1** shows participation rates in four sports between May 2012 and August 2012. (1)

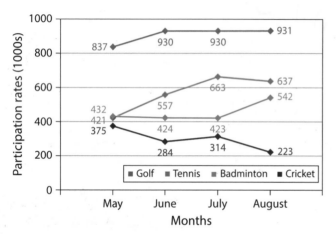

▲ **Figure 1**

Using **Figure 1**, identify the sport with the greatest increase in participation between May and June.
   - **A** Golf
   - **B** Badminton
   - **C** Tennis
   - **D** Cricket

3. Which one from the following is **not** an ethical or socio-cultural factor affecting performance? (1)
   - **A** Disability
   - **B** Ethnicity
   - **C** Gender
   - **D** Optimum weight

4. Which of the following is **not** an effect of ageing on performance? (1)
   - **A** Tidal volume and stroke volume increase with age
   - **B** Flexibility decreases with age
   - **C** Experience increases with age
   - **D** It takes longer to recover from injury with age

5. Complete the following statements about the impact of the behaviour of elite performers on sport. (2)
   ............................................ behaviour goes against the moral values or rules of a sport. It can have a negative effect on the sporting community and on wider society. Elite athletes are often seen as role models. It is, therefore, important that they demonstrate ............................................ and model the values of fair play.

6. Using sport examples, describe the difference between sportsmanship and gamesmanship. (4)

7. Sport England's 2014/15 survey reports that 54.8% of 16- to 25-year-olds take part in at least one sport session a week, compared to 31.9% of older adults (26 plus).
   Explain two ways in which age influences participation rates. (4)

8. Many elite athletes benefit from the commercialisation of sport.
   Explain why media coverage is beneficial for a performer. (4)

9. Evaluate the importance of commercialisation in improving sport for the spectator. (9)

10. Sport England aims to increase participation rates in sport and physical activity among all groups in society by removing the barriers to participation. Using examples, evaluate the factors that have an impact on participation rates. (9)

# 7 Practical Performance and Personal Exercise Programme (PEP)

When you have worked through this chapter, you will have developed knowledge and understanding of:

- what is required for the practical performance component of the course (30% of your overall mark)

- how to go about planning, carrying out and evaluating a Personal Exercise Programme (PEP) (worth 10% of your overall mark).

This component assesses your performance in three different physical activities throughout your course. Your total mark is worth 30% of your overall grade.

You must choose **three** activities from the list provided by Edexcel. You must choose:

- one team activity

- one individual activity

- one activity of your choice, either team or individual.

It is important to know where your strengths currently lie and to use this information to think about possible combinations of physical activities. However, while it's a good idea to have thought about your possible combinations, it is sensible not to rule other activities out. You may surprise yourself and end up with a different combination that earns you more marks.

If one or more of the activities on your list of three possible options is not delivered at school, you must plan ahead and work out when and how you will gain video evidence of your performance. You should speak to your PE teacher about this.

▲ For example, you could combine netball (team activity), singles tennis (individual activity) and football (choice). This kind of combination would obviously suit a good games player.

▲ For example, you could combine doubles badminton (team activity), swimming (individual activity) and dance (choice). This kind of combination would suit someone who excels in more individualised activities.

For each activity, you will be assessed on your ability to perform:

- the skills that make up the activity

- your general performance within competitive situations.

It is very likely that your teacher will assess you in many more than three activities to allow you to find your highest scoring combination. This means you should try your very best in every activity in every lesson to ensure that the marks you receive, in both isolated and competitive situations, demonstrate your full potential. Every extra mark will increase your chance of achieving the grade you want overall.

At the end of the course, you may be selected to attend moderation. This means that the marks given by your teachers are checked to ensure they line up with the marks given by other teachers at other schools for performances of similar quality. If you are selected to be moderated, it is imperative that you do your very best.

## Activity

1. **a)** Look through the lists of team and individual activities in the Edexcel specification and consider which activities you are actively involved in on a regular basis.

   **b)** Think back to Key Stage 3 and reflect on your performance in activities you had access to there. Which activities did you improve in most over the three years? Which did you enjoy most? Which did you find most challenging?

   **c)** Find out from your teacher if there are likely to be any new activities offered in Key Stage 4 that you might perform well in.

   **d)** Look at the assessment criteria for the activities you are considering.

   **e)** With the help of your peers and teachers, create several possible combinations that could allow you to access the highest possible number of marks.

This component assesses your skills in analysing and evaluating your performance during a six- to eight-week Personal Exercise Programme, often referred to as a 'PEP'. Your PEP must be designed to improve or optimise your performance in a physical activity or sport from the list provided by Edexcel. Your total mark is worth 10% of your overall grade.

Your PEP can be presented either through a written analysis and evaluation or through a verbal presentation that is videoed. It is likely that your teacher will decide which is the best option because they have the knowledge and experience to know which method will allow you to achieve your best, and which method is most suitable for the school.

### Exam tip

In almost all cases, your PEP should be linked to your main sporting activity, as this is the activity that you will know most about. If this decision is a difficult one for you, you should talk to your teacher about which activity will give you the best opportunity to produce a strong PEP. Throughout this chapter the chosen activity will be referred to as the "linked activity".

In the presentation of your PEP, you will:

- outline the aim of your PEP and analyse your planning stage

- demonstrate how you carried out and monitored your PEP

- evaluate the data produced and the programme itself.

To do this successfully, you will need to show knowledge of the principles of training, relevant methods of training and use of data. You will build knowledge of all of these during your GCSE course, and you should always be thinking about how the theory you are learning links with practical performance in general and especially your PEP.

### Exam tip

In order to achieve the maximum number of marks that you are capable of, you should begin your PEP by reading 'Component 4: Personal Exercise Programme (PEP)' in the specification. You should also look closely at the PEP assessment criteria, paying particular attention to your target level, which your teacher may help you in choosing.

To assist you in the execution and documentation of your PEP, the process will now be mapped out for you, step by step:

## Preparation

Complete a Physical Activity Readiness Questionnaire (PARQ) which will detail your individual needs and personal medical information. This will be important in helping you plan a suitable and safe PEP.

## Selection ②

Decide on the physical activity or sport that your PEP will link to and conduct an analysis of the requirements of your linked activity. Identify one component of fitness that you feel is a) important to your linked activity and b) an area that you would benefit from improving. Choose from: cardiovascular fitness, strength, muscular endurance, flexibility, body composition, agility, balance, coordination, power, reaction time and speed.

### Exam tip

Some components of fitness are better suited to a PEP than others. You should consider which component of fitness you feel you are able to improve through the training methods you understand and have access to equipment for.

## Pre-testing ③

Having chosen your linked activity and the appropriate component of fitness, you will need to do a pre-PEP fitness test to see where you currently are, ahead of completing the exercise programme. You must consider which recognised test links most closely to your chosen component of fitness. The idea is that you re-test at the end of the programme so that you can measure the improvements made.

Information on the recognised tests for each component of fitness are discussed on pages 59–74.

### Exam tip

In addition to identifying a suitable component of fitness, an excellent PEP will also consider the major muscle groups that are used in the activity and the types of movements that are used most often.

## Pre-test analysis ④

Analyse your pre-PEP fitness test data and decide which method of training you are going to use in your PEP to develop your chosen component of fitness. You will need to justify why you have chosen that method of training and why you feel it will be more beneficial to you than others available.

Information on methods of training can be found on pages 83–89.

### Exam tip

You can choose to do more than one fitness test and to use more than one method of training if you wish, but you should only plan to include things that tie closely to your chosen component of fitness, your linked activity and your goals.

## Goal setting ⑤

Using the principles of SMART targets, set yourself some goals that revolve around the overall aim of your PEP; what you would like to gain from executing it. Think about the improvements you hope to make in your chosen component of fitness and the impact you hope these improvements will make on your performance in your linked activity.

## Planning

You will need to think about and justify how you will use the principles of training throughout your PEP. Remember that following the principles of training ensures that training is effective, so it is really important to consider them heavily in your planning. How will your training meet your individual needs; apply specificity, progressive overload and rest and recovery; avoid reversibility; and use the FITT principle and thresholds of training?

You should decide how many sessions a week you will do, what the content of those sessions will be, what intensities you'll start at and how the intensity will change during the PEP. You should also think about how you'll gather evidence throughout the PEP to assist you in your analysis at the end.

More information about the principles of training can be found on page 75.

## Recording

Create a template that allows you to record your training and progress. This can then be used in conjunction with the "Personal exercise programme training record form" provided by Edexcel in the specification. You'll need to keep continuous records of your work as you move through the six to eight week PEP, as well as consider how you may want to present the information at the end.

## Exam tip

You should have a plan of what you are going to do, a record of what you did do and data for every session in your six- to eight-week PEP, along with any thoughts about the strengths and weaknesses of your plan and changes that you made during the sessions.

## Collect data

While completing your exercise sessions during the six- to eight-week PEP, you will need to collect data. What data you collect will depend on the component of fitness you have selected. For example, if you have chosen cardiovascular fitness you will need to measure your heart rate (at rest, during exercise and during recovery). If you have chosen muscular endurance you will need to record repetitions, sets and recovery time between sets. If you have chosen strength will need to record weight/resistance used.

## Re-test (9)

At the end of the PEP, you should carry out exactly the same fitness test that you performed at the beginning and record the results.

## Pre-test/re-test analysis (10)

What is the difference between the pre-test results and the re-test results? What does this tell you? Did you meet your goals? How will this impact your performance in your linked activity?

## Presenting your PEP data (11)

You will now have lots of data, some quantitative and some qualitative. You'll need to present this in effective ways to help you review the quality of your PEP and the impact it has had. You should include some graphs, charts, tables and diagrams alongside explanations of what they show and what this information tells you. You're presenting, interpreting and evaluating.

## Reflect on and evaluate your PEP (12)

Using all your plans and records and all the data you have, you now need to evaluate your PEP. You need to consider the overall effectiveness of the programme in developing your chosen component of fitness and its impact on your performance in your linked activity. How has it all gone? Would you change anything if you planned it again? Did anything get in the way of your expected progress? Do you feel the PEP has been effective? How has it made you a better performer? Did you meet your goals?

## The next steps (13)

Finish by outlining briefly which strategies you would employ if you were continuing your PEP. What is now important in taking your performance in your linked activity to the next level? Would you target another important component of fitness? Would you use different methods of training to get different improvements? How would you move your training on again?

## Submit and sign (14)

Submit all your work to your teacher and help them to ensure that your "Personal exercise programme (PEP) authentication sheet" is filled accurately with all your details. This is likely to become the front sheet for your work. You'll need to sign, as the candidate, to say that the work is all your own.

# Glossary

## A

**Aerobic training target zone** 60–80% of your maximum heart rate.

**Aerobic work** Working at a moderate intensity so that the body has time to use oxygen for energy production and can work for a continuous period of time. For example, long-distance events, for the duration of a match.

**Agility** A measure of how quickly you can change the position of your body, while keeping your entire body under control.

**Agonist** The muscle within the pair that, at a given time, is contracting to pull on the bone and produce movement.

**Anaerobic training target zone** 80–90% of your maximum heart rate.

**Anaerobic work** Working at a high intensity without oxygen for energy production. The work period will be short in duration, because the energy is limited. For example, sprinting up the wing in a football match.

**Antagonist** The muscle within the pair that, at a given time, is relaxing to allow movement to occur.

**Antagonistic muscle pair** A pair of muscles that work together to produce movement. As one muscle contracts (agonist), the other relaxes (antagonist). For example, the biceps and triceps. The triceps relax to allow the biceps to contract to flex the arm at the elbow. Roles are reversed to extend the arm at the elbow.

**Aorta** The artery that carries blood from the heart to the rest of the body.

**Arteries** Blood vessels that carry oxygenated blood from the heart to muscles and organs.

**Atria** This is the plural for "atrium". There are two atria in the heart. These are the upper chambers of the heart where blood enters.

**Axis** An imaginary line around which a body or body part can turn. "Axes" is the plural of axis.

## B

**Balance** Your ability to keep your body steady, both when in a static position and when moving.

**Basic skill** A simple skill requiring little concentration to execute.

**Bicuspid valve** A one-way gate that separates the left atrium from the left ventricle.

**Body composition** A measure of the percentages of fat, muscle, bone, water and vital organs that make up your body weight.

## C

**Capillaries** Blood vessels that wrap around muscles and organs so that gaseous exchange can take place.

**Carbohydrate** Fuel for aerobic and anaerobic activity. Carbohydrate sources include rice, pasta and bread.

**Carbohydrate loading** A strategy used by endurance athletes to boost glycogen stores before a competition.

**Cardiac equation** stroke volume × heart rate = cardiac output (SV × HR = Q)

**Cardiac muscle** The muscle of the heart, which pumps blood around the body.

**Cardiac output (Q)** The volume of blood pumped out of the heart per minute, measured in litres per minute (l/min).

**Cardio-respiratory system** The name given to the combined body system that involves your cardiovascular system and your respiratory system.

**Cardiovascular fitness (aerobic endurance)** A measure of how efficiently your body can deliver oxygen and nutrients, such as glucose, to your working muscles during exercise, and also carry away waste products, such as carbon dioxide and lactic acid.

**Cardiovascular system** the heart, blood vessels and blood.

**Class of lever** The type of lever. There are first class, second class and third class levers.

**Classifications of bone** The bone classification tells you a lot about its structure. A bone's classification will also link closely to its major functions.

**Classifications of joints** There are four main classifications of joint: pivot joints, hinge joints, ball and socket joints and condyloid joints. Each type of joint has a specific range of movement.

**Closed skill** A skill performed in a predictable environment. For example, a player taking a penalty.

**Commercialisation** The commercialisation of physical activity and sport involves individuals, organisations and companies buying and selling sporting goods and services with a focus on profit rather than participation.

**Complex skill** A skill requiring a lot of attention and concentration.

**Concurrent feedback** Information a performer receives about their performance during the activity.

**Continuum** A line with a classification extreme at each end. Skills can then be placed on the continuum; the closer they are placed to the extreme, the more like that extreme they are.

**Contraction** A muscle contracts when it is activated and tension is created. Muscles shorten and pull when they contract; they don't push.

**Coordination** The ability to move two or more body parts together, accurately and smoothly.

# D

**Deoxygenated blood** Blood containing a low concentration of oxygen.

**Deviant behaviour** Behaviour that goes against the moral values or rules of a sport.

**Diffusion** The term used to describe how molecules move from an area of higher concentration to an area of lower concentration in an attempt to reach a balance.

**Distributed practice** Intervals between skill practice in a training session for rest or mental rehearsal.

**Duration** How long something lasts.

# E

**Effort** The source of the energy. For example, muscles in the body.

**Effort arm** The distance from the effort to the fulcrum.

**Energy** The capacity to do work.

**Energy balance** This is the basis of weight control. For body weight to remain constant energy input (via food) must equal energy expenditure.

**Exercise** A form of physical activity done to maintain or improve health and/or fitness; it is not a competitive sport.

**Exhale** We exhale air when we breathe out. The process of exhaling is called "exhalation".

**Extrinsic feedback** Information a performer receives about their performance from a coach.

# F

**Fat** Fuel for aerobic activity. Sources of fat include butter and oil.

**Fatty acids** Fats are converted into fatty acids, which are used as fuel in energy production.

**Feedback** Information received during or after a performance about the performance.

**Fitness** The ability to meet the demands of the environment.

**FITT** This stands for **F**requency, **I**ntensity, **T**ime and **T**ype. The FITT principle should be used to ensure that a Personal Exercise Programme (PEP) delivers progressive overload.

**Fixed practice** Repeatedly practising a whole skill within a training session.

**Flexibility** The ability of your joints to move through their full range of movement.

**Frequency (f)** The number of breaths taken per minute, measured in breaths. It is also referred to as your "rate of breathing".

**Frontal axis** An imaginary line passing horizontally through the body from left to right, allowing flexion and extension.

**Frontal plane** An imaginary line dividing the body vertically from front to back. Movement occurs in the frontal plane about the sagittal axis. For example, when performing a star jump.

**Fulcrum** A fixed pivot point. For example, a joint in the body.

**Functions of the cardiovascular system** The three functions of the cardiovascular system are transport, clotting and temperature regulation.

**Functions of the skeleton** The skeleton performs five important functions. These are: protection of vital organs, muscle attachment, joints for movement, blood cell production, and mineral storage.

# G

**Gamesmanship** Bending the rules/laws of a sport without actually breaking them.

**Gaseous exchange** Once the alveoli in the lungs have filled with air, gaseous exchange takes place. Oxygen moves from the air in the alveoli into the blood in the capillaries, while carbon dioxide moves from the blood in the capillaries into the air in the alveoli.

**Glucose** Carbohydrates are converted into glucose, which is used as a fuel in energy production.

**Goal setting** The process of setting down targets that a performer will aim to accomplish.

**Grassroots participation** This is participation in sport and physical activity that takes place at the local level. It often involves lots of volunteers who organise and coach training sessions and competitions for the love of the sport.

**Guidance** Information to aid the learning of a skill.

# H

**Health** A state of complete emotional, physical and social well-being, and not merely the absence of disease and infirmity.

**Heart rate (HR)** The number of heart beats per minute, measured in beats per minute (bpm).

**High organisation skill** A skill that cannot be broken down easily and practised separately because the phases of the skill are closely linked. For example, a cartwheel or a golf swing.

**Hydration** Being hydrated means your body contains the correct amount of water in its cells, tissues and organs to function correctly. If you do not have enough water in your body you are "dehydrated". The average recommended daily intake is 2.5 litres of water for men and 2 litres for women.

# I

**Inhale** We inhale air when we breathe in. The process of inhaling is called "inhalation".

**Intensity** How relatively powerful something is.

**Intrinsic feedback** Information a performer receives about their performance that comes from within and is linked to how a movement feels.

**Involuntary muscle** The muscle involved in digestion and vascular shunting.

# K

**Karvonen formula** Target Heart Rate = ((MHR − RHR) × %Intensity) + RHR. (MHR = Maximum Heart Rate calculated as 220 − age. RHR = Resting Heart Rate.)

# L

**Lactate accumulation** The name given to the process of lactic acid accumulating within the blood and muscles due to increased work intensity. For example, when moving from aerobic to anaerobic exercise.

**Lactic acid** A by-product of energy production, which is formed when the body is exercising anaerobically at high intensity. A build up of lactic acid results in muscle fatigue.

**Lever** A rigid bar or object that moves around a fixed fulcrum with two forces applied to it.

**Lifestyle choices** The choices we make about how we live and behave that impact on our health.

**Ligament** Connective tissue that attaches bone to bone at joints. Its role is to prevent dislocation.

**Load** The weight/resistance to be moved. For example, a body part plus anything held or resistance met.

**Load arm** The distance from the load to the fulcrum.

**Low organisation skill** A basic skill that can be broken down easily into different phases so each part can be practised separately. For example, a tennis serve or the front crawl swimming stroke.

**Lumen** The internal diameter of a blood vessel.

# M

**Macronutrients** Nutrients that you need to consume in relatively large amounts in order to eat a balanced diet. These are carbohydrates, proteins and fats.

**Manual guidance** Information given to a performer to help them develop that involves them being physically moved into the correct position.

**Massed practice** Practice that occurs without breaks between trials (practice attempts).

**Mechanical advantage** Second class levers allow a large load to be moved with a relatively small amount of muscular effort.

**Mechanical disadvantage** Third class levers cannot lift such heavy loads, with the same amount of effort, as second class levers due to the position of the fulcrum in relation to the effort and load.

**Mechanical guidance** Information given to a performer to help them develop that involves equipment to assist in the learning process. For example, using a harness in trampolining.

**Mental rehearsal** Practising the skill in your head before actually doing it.

**Micronutrients** Nutrients that you need to consume in relatively small amounts in order to eat a balanced diet. These include vitamins and minerals.

**Minute ventilation** The amount of air inhaled or exhaled per minute, measured in litres (l).

**Movement types** Names used to identify directions of movement at joints. These include flexion, extension, adduction, abduction, rotation, circumduction, plantar-flexion and dorsi-flexion.

**Muscle fatigue** A reduction in a muscle's ability to produce force.

**Muscle fibre types** Every voluntary muscle in the body contains thousands of muscle fibres. The different fibre types are type I, type IIa and type IIx.

**Muscular endurance** A measure of the length of time your voluntary muscles can contract without getting tired. This can be repeated muscle contractions, or one contraction held for a long period of time.

**Musculo-skeletal system** The name given to the combined body system that involves your muscles and your skeleton.

# N

**Normative data** Normative data shows the results for "normal" people. Data is collected from a large sample of people and the "most common" results are established.

# O

**Obese** Weighing significantly more than the ideal weight for your height and having an excess amount of body fat.

**Open skill** A skill performed in an unpredictable environment, where the performer has to react and adjust to the changing nature of the situation. For example, a player trying to pass the ball to a team mate who is trying to get free from the opposition.

**Optimum weight** Refers to the weight someone should be, on average, based on their sex, height, bone structure and muscle girth.

**Overfat** Having more than the ideal amount of body fat.

**Overtraining** This occurs when you train too hard and do not give your body enough time to rest and recover between training sessions.

**Overweight** Weighing more than the ideal weight for your height.

**Oxygenated blood** Blood containing a high concentration of oxygen.

# P

**PARQ** Stands for **P**hysical **A**ctivity **R**eadiness **Q**uestionnaire.

**Performance** The action of performing a task, including a sporting performance.

**Plane** An imaginary line dividing the body into two.

**Plasma** The liquid element of blood that allows it to flow.

**Platelets** These clot blood at the site of a wound.

**Power** The ability to combine strength with speed to perform a strong muscular contraction very quickly.

**Principles of training** Guidelines that, if applied, ensure that training is effective and results in positive adaptations. The principles of training are: individual needs, specificity, progressive overload (FITT), overtraining and reversibility.

**Progressive overload** The frequency, intensity, time and/or type of exercise are gradually increased to ensure that levels of fitness continue to improve.

**Psychological warm-up** A performer gets mentally ready to give their very best.

**Pulmonary artery** The artery that carries deoxygenated blood from the heart to the lungs.

**Pulmonary vein** The vein that carries oxygenated blood from the lungs to the heart.

# Q

**Qualitative data** Data that focuses on understanding things; it involves detailed information about the way people think and behave.

**Quantitative data** Data that focuses on measuring things; it involves numbers.

# R

**Range of movement** Different joints allow different movements to take place. Joints that can perform many different types of movements have a large range of movement.

**Reaction time** The amount of time it takes you to respond to a stimulus.

**Red blood cells** These contain haemoglobin, which carries oxygen.

**Respiratory equation** tidal volume $\times$ frequency = minute ventilation (TV $\times$ f = VE).

**Reversibility** Any adaptations made as a result of training will be reversed if training stops.

## S

**Sagittal axis** An imaginary line passing horizontally through the body from front to back, allowing abduction and adduction.

**Sagittal plane** An imaginary line dividing the body vertically into left and right sides. Movement occurs in the sagittal plane around the frontal axis. For example, when performing a somersault.

**Sedentary lifestyle** A lifestyle where there is little, irregular or no physical activity.

**Semi-lunar valves** One-way gates at the entrance to the aorta and pulmonary artery, which prevent the backflow of the blood into the heart.

**Skill** A skill in physical activity is a specific and defined task that can be learned and practised.

**SMART targets** An acronym used to guide the setting of effective goals. SMART targets are **S**pecific, **M**easurable, **A**chievable, **R**ealistic and **T**ime-bound.

**Specificity** Training should be matched to the requirements of the activity that the performer is involved in.

**Speed** The rate at which your body, or part of your body, is able to perform a movement.

**Sportsmanship** The qualities of fairness, following the rules and being gracious in defeat or victory.

**Strength** The amount of force a muscle can generate when it contracts to overcome resistance.

**Stroke Volume (SV)** The amount of blood pumped out of the heart per beat, measured in millilitres per heart beat (ml/beat).

## T

**Tendon** Connective tissue that attaches muscle to bone. Its role is to transfer the effort created by a contracting muscle to the bone, resulting in the movement of that bone.

**Terminal feedback** Information a performer receives about their performance after the activity has been completed.

**Tidal volume (TV)** The amount of air inhaled or exhaled per breath, measured in millilitres (ml). It is also referred to as your "depth of breathing".

**Transverse plane** An imaginary line dividing the body horizontally from front to back. Movement occurs in the transverse plane around the vertical axis. For example, when performing a full twist jump.

**Tricuspid valve** A one-way gate that separates the right atrium from the right ventricle.

**Type I muscle fibres** These are also known as slow twitch muscle fibres. Type I muscle fibres are suited to low intensity aerobic work such as marathon running because they can be used for a long time without fatiguing.

**Type IIa muscle fibres** These are fast twitch fibres. They are suited to lengthy anaerobic work, such as an 800 m race, and can be improved through endurance training to increase their resistance to fatigue.

**Type IIx muscle fibres** These are fast twitch muscle fibres. They are used in anaerobic work and can generate much greater force than the other muscle fibre types, but they fatigue quickly. They are beneficial to 100 m sprinters. In the past, this type of muscle fibre has been referred to as "type IIb".

## V

**Variable practice** A training session that includes frequent changes of task so that the skill can be repeated in different situations.

**Vascular shunting** A process that increases blood flow to active areas during exercise by diverting blood away from inactive areas. This is achieved by vasoconstriction and vasodilation.

**Vasoconstriction** The narrowing of the internal diameter (lumen) of a blood vessel to decrease blood flow.

**Vasodilation** The widening of the internal diameter (lumen) of a blood vessel to increase blood flow.

**Veins** Blood vessels that carry deoxygenated blood from muscles and organs to the heart.

**Vena cava** The large vein entering the right atrium of the heart that carries deoxygenated blood back from the body to the heart. There is an inferior vena cava and a superior vena cava.

**Ventricles** There are two ventricles in the heart. These are the lower chambers of the heart from where blood exits.

**Verbal guidance** Information given to a performer to help them develop that they can hear. It involves someone telling them something. For example, a coach explaining how to perform a technique.

**Vertical axis** An imaginary line passing vertically through the body, allowing rotation of the body in an upright position.

**Visual guidance** Information given to a performer to help them develop that they can see. For example, through demonstrations.

**Vital capacity** The maximum amount of air exhaled following a maximum inhalation.

**Voluntary muscle** Muscle involved in skeletal movement.

# W

**Well-being** A general term used to describe a state of physical, emotional and social health.

**White blood cells** These blood cells fight infections and diseases.

# Index

# OXFORD
## UNIVERSITY PRESS

Great Clarendon Street, Oxford, OX2 6DP, United Kingdom

Oxford University Press is a department of the University of Oxford.

It furthers the University's objective of excellence in research, scholarship, and education by publishing worldwide. Oxford is a registered trade mark of Oxford University Press in the UK and in certain other countries

British Library Cataloguing in Publication Data
Data available

978-0-19-837021-5

10 9 8 7 6 5 4 3 2

Paper used in the production of this book is a natural, recyclable product made from wood grown in sustainable forests. The manufacturing process conforms to the environmental regulations of the country of origin.

Printed in China by Golden Cup

## Acknowledgements

The publishers would like to thank the following for permissions to use their photographs:

p5: SEBASTIAN KAULITZKI/Science Photo Library/Corbis; p7: NATIONAL CANCER INSTITUTE/SCIENCE PHOTO LIBRARY; p7: Ben Hoskins/Getty Images; p10: Stu Forster/ Getty Images; p10: TOBY MELVILLE/Reuters/Corbis; p10: STOYAN NENOV/Reuters/ Corbis; p10: ZURAB KURTSIKIDZE/epa/Corbis; p10: Andy Buchanan/AFP/Getty Images; p10: Joosep Martinson - ISU/ISU via Getty Images; p13: K Asif/India Today Group/Getty Images; p14: Yegor Aleyev/ITAR-TASS Photo/Corbis; p15: badmintonphoto.com; p15: Clint Hughes - The FA via Getty Images; p17: Gonzalo Arroyo Moreno/Getty Images for FIVB; p18: Doug Pensinger/Getty Images; p19: DR. GLADDEN WILLIS, VISUALS UNLIMITED /SCIENCE PHOTO LIBRARY; p20: Jean Catuffe/Getty Images; p20: Ian Walton/Getty Images; p21: Michael Steele/Getty Images; p23: ANIMATED HEALTHCARE LTD/SCIENCE PHOTO LIBRARY; p23: Ammentorp Photography / Alamy; p28: POWER AND SYRED/SCIENCE PHOTO LIBRARY; p28: JACKY NAEGELEN/Reuters/Corbis; p28: STEVE GSCHMEISSNER/SCIENCE PHOTO LIBRARY; p28: MBI / Alamy Stock Photo; p29: NIBSC/SCIENCE PHOTO LIBRARY; p29: Colorsport/Corbis; p34: sam bloomberg-rissman /Blend Images / Alamy; p34: sam bloomberg-rissman /Blend Images / Alamy; p36: Julian Finney/Getty Images; p36: blickwinkel / Alamy Stock Photo; p38: Nerthuz/ Shutterstock; p40: Nerthuz/Shutterstock; p40: BURGER/PHANIE/phanie/ Phanie Sarl /Corbis; p42: Eraxion/iStockphoto; p44: FCG/ Shutterstock; p45: Cal Sport Media / Alamy Stock Photo; p45: VALDRIN XHEMAJ/epa/Corbis; p47: Bohemian Nomad Picturemakers/CORBIS; p49: Ole Graf/Corbis; p49: omgimages/iStockphoto; p49: Anderson Ross/ Getty; p50: Stock Foundry Images / Alamy ; p51: FABRICE COFFRINI/ AFP/Getty Images; p51: Harry How/Getty Images; p52: Faye Clack/Roddy Clark; p52: Faye Clack/Roddy Clark; p53: Ellie Faulkner/Roddy Clark; p54: Markku Ulander/ REX Shutterstock; p54: Faye Clack/Roddy Clark; p55: Max Ellis Photography; p59: JEFF PACHOUD/AFP/Getty Images; p62: Greg Epperson/ Shutterstock; p63: SUZANNE PLUNKETT/Reuters/Corbis; p63: blickwinkel / Alamy Stock Photo; p66: Erik Isakson/ Rubberball/Corbis; p67: Giuliano Bevilacqua/Corbis; p67: DYLAN MARTINEZ/Reuters/ Corbis; p68: Francois Nel/Getty Images; p69: Joe Toth/BPI/Corbis; p69: PCN/Corbis;

p70: Jason Winslow/Splash News/Corbis; p71: Stuart Hannagan/Getty Images; p72: Boris Streubel/Getty Images; p74: Richard Heathcote/Getty Images; p77: ALLSTAR Picture Library / Alamy; p77: epa european pressphoto agency b.v. / Alamy; p81: Dirima/ Shutterstock; p82: Matthew Peters/Manchester United via Getty Images; p83: John Giles/ PA Archive/Press Association Images; p85: Bradley Ormesher/The Times/ News Syndication; p85: Dean Drobot/ Shutterstock; p85: Mihai Blanaru/ Shutterstock; p85: kjekol/iStockphoto; p86: John Giles/ PA Archive/ PA images; p88: Peter Bernik/ Shutterstock; p88: wavebreakmedia/ Shutterstock; p88: skynesher/iStockphoto; p89: YanLev/Shutterstock; p89: wavebreakmedia/ Shutterstock; p92: Justin Setterfield/ Getty Images; p94: Monkey Business Images/ Shutterstock; p94: Preston Keres/The Washington Post/Getty Images; p95: Wade Eakle/ Getty; p95: Sandra Mu/Getty Images; p95: Adam Gasson / Alamy; p95: Tino Soriano/National Geographic Creative/Corbis; p96: Tony Marshall/Getty Images; p97: Puwadol Jaturawutthichai/ Shutterstock; p97: Clive Brunskill/Getty Images; p98: Bob Martin/Sports Illustrated/Getty Images; p98: lzf/iStockphoto; p99: Science Photo Library; p99: TR/AFP/Getty Images; p100: Robert Laberge/Getty Images; p103: GLYN KIRK/AFP/Getty Images; p103: MIGUEL MEDINA/ AFP/Getty Images); p104: Matthew Lewis/Getty Images; p105: Eliza Snow/ Getty Images; p105: Peter Muller/Corbis; p107: Monkey Business Images/ Shutterstock; p110: Raisman/ Shutterstock; p110: Ed Bock/CORBIS; p111: Aleksandr Markin/ Shutterstock; p111: Digoarpi/ Shutterstock; p112: photographee.eu/ Shutterstock; p114: racorn/Shutterstock; p115: Istvan Csak/ Shutterstock; p116: fcafotodigital/ iStockphoto; p116: worker/Shutterstock; p117: Andresr/ Shutterstock; p117: esolla/ Shutterstock; p117: photographee.eu/ Shutterstock; p117: monkeybusinessimages/ iStockphoto ; p118: Les Gibbon / Alamy; p119: Arthur Glauberman/SCIENCE PHOTO LIBRARY; p120: ranplett/iStockphoto; p120: AndreasReh/iStockphoto; p120: Mark Hayes / Alamy; p123: Courtesy of the Food Standards Agency; p124: 5 second Studio/ Shutterstock; p124: Heidi van der Westhuizen/ iStockphoto; p124: Stephen Chung / Alamy; p125: Africa Studio/ Shutterstock; p125: IGOR KOVALENKO/epa/Corbis; p126: redmal/ iStockphoto; p126: Tina Larsson/ Shutterstock; p126: shakzu/iStockphoto; p126: Olga Besnard/ Shutterstock; p127: auremar/ Shutterstock; p127: Creativeye99/ iStockphoto; p128: Maxisport/ Shutterstock; p128: Robyn Mackenzie/ Shutterstock; p130: HECTOR RETAMAL/AFP/Getty Images; p130: JIM WATSON/AFP/Getty Images); p130: PRAKASH SINGH/AFP/Getty Images; p130: Timothy A. Clary/AFP/Getty; p130: Fred Beckham/ AP / PA Images; p130: The Asahi Shimbun via Getty Images); p131: Hannah Peters/Getty Images; p131: Julian Herbert/Getty Images); p133: ANDY RAIN/epa/Corbis; p134: Rob Griffith/ AP Photo/ PA; p134: Charlie Crowhurst/Getty Images; p135: KERIM OKTEN/EPA/Corbis; p135: Brendon Thorne/Getty Images; p136: Paul Gilham/Getty Images; p136: BEN STANSALL/AFP/Getty Images; p137: FRANCOIS XAVIER MARIT/ AFP/Getty Images; p137: Patrick Smith/Getty Images); p138: Lida DeGroote /J and L Photography/Getty Images; p139: Michael Regan/Getty Images; p140: Warren Little/ Getty Images; p141: Gabriel Rossi/LatinContent/Getty Images; p142: KAZUHIRO NOGI/ AFP/Getty Images); p143: Sarunyu_foto/ Shutterstock; p144: Jean Catuffe/Getty Images; p145: Pressmaster/ Shutterstock; p145: salez/ iStockphoto; p145: Therese McKeon/ iStockphoto; p145: Sky_Blue/ iStockphoto; p145: Joe Murphy/NBAE via Getty Images); p146: Zero Creatives/Getty Images; p147: Bill McCay/WireImage/ Getty; p148: Picture Perfect/REX Shutterstock; p150: SAEED KHAN/AFP/Getty Images; p150: INDRANIL MUKHERJEE/AFP/Getty Images); p150: Danny Lawson/ PA Archive/Press Association Images; p150: Cameron Spencer/Getty Images); p151: Courtesy of Hawkeye; p152: Alex Livesey/Getty Images; p153: Paul Gilham/Getty Images; p153: TOBY MELVILLE/Reuters/ Corbis; p153: Visionhaus/Corbis; p153: Montana Pritchard/The PGA of America via Getty Images); p154: ANDY RAIN/epa/Corbis; p155: Michael Cole/Corbis; p156 & 158 & 160 & 161 & 163: Courtesy of Sport England; p157: David Dow/NBAE via Getty Images; p158: Courtesy of Sport England 'This Girl Can' Campaign; p158: Christopher Futcher/ Getty Images; p159: Craig Lassig/Invision for Humana/AP Images/ PA; p160: Paul Springett A / Alamy; p161: Ben Radford/Getty Images; p162: STOYAN NENOV/Reuters/ Corbis; p162: Al Bello/Getty Images; p162: Andy Buchanan/AFP/Getty Images; p162: Ben Queenborough/BPI/REX Shutterstock; p163: Clive Rose/Getty Images; p166: Gareth Copley/Getty Images; p167: Bryn Lennon/Getty Images; p167: SERGEI ILNITSKY/epa/ Corbis; p168: INPHO/Tommy Grealy; p168: GLYN KIRK/AFP/Getty Images; p169: Gareth Copley/Getty Images; p169: Harry How/Getty Images; p170: Eric Gaillard/Reuters/ Corbis; p170: Bob Thomas/Getty Images; p170: STF/AFP/Getty Images; p171: YASUYOSHI CHIBA/AFP/Getty Images; p173: Aviva/ Getty Images; p174: ALAN EDWARDS / Alamy ; p174: Galina Barskaya/ Shutterstock; p174: strickke/iStockphoto; p175: James Davies / Alamy; p175: jabejon/iStockphoto; p175: AYakovlev/ iStockphoto; p177: BreatheFitness/ iStockphoto; p178-179: monkeybusinessimages/ iStockphoto.

Artwork by OUP and MPS Ltd.

Thank you to the staff at Roundwood Park School and to Indexing Specialists (UK) Ltd for the index.

Although we have made every effort to trace and contact all copyright holders before publication this has not been possible in all cases. If notified, the publisher will rectify any errors or omissions at the earliest opportunity.